FAIR CHASE

WITH ALASKAN GUIDES

FAIR
CHASE
WITH ALASKAN GUIDES

BY HAL WAUGH AND CHARLES J. KEIM

ALASKA NORTHWEST PUBLISHING COMPANY
Anchorage, Alaska
1972

Printed in U. S. A.

Library of Congress Number: 72-83636

International Standard Book Number
0-88240-010-X

Cover photo by Jim Rearden, ALASKA® magazine

DEDICATION

TO
Our Alaskan Partners
Julie and Betty
and
in Memory of
Dr. Ivar Skarland

CONTENTS

INTRODUCTION

Long before the first explorers began penetrating The North Country, the native inhabitants had discovered its worth and appropriately had named it "Alaska," meaning "The Great Land."

Today, in an era of increasing environmental concern, the name means something different to every Alaskan. Inevitably their evaluation includes in varying degrees an appreciation of the vastness of the land and what it encompasses—the great valleys, mountains, forests, tundra covered plains, lakes, rivers and seas and all their varied inhabitants, both human and animal.

Fortunate indeed is the Alaskan who can arrange his life to enjoy in even greater measure the Alaska outdoors, utilizing it in a fair chase spirit, yet helping to assure that his sons and theirs will have these same opportunities.

Even more fortunate is the Alaskan who can enjoy The Great Land in the company of like-minded companions who recognize God's hand in the beauty of a frost-touched hillside; the dimpling of a quiet lake by a trout or grayling; a sunrise or sunset firing snow-capped peaks with color far beyond man's poor ability to capture with brush or camera; a Dall sheep silhouetted against that sky; or even the tantalizing aroma of early morning coffee nudging sleepy hunters, fishermen or camera enthusiasts into zestful wakefulness and refreshed ability to enjoy this beauty and meet The North Country's challenges, whether with gun, rod or camera.

We count ourselves especially fortunate to have undergone such experiences and to have shared them in the field with others. We sincerely hope that FAIR CHASE WITH ALASKAN GUIDES will help some readers recall pleasant outdoor experiences and that it will enable those who have not yet enjoyed The Great Land at least to do so vicariously.

H. W.
C. J. K.

x

Kodiak's Lucky Knoll

The camera angle emphasizes the size of this "Lucky Knoll" brownie, but guide Hal Waugh knows all big brownies weigh over half a ton.

1

Story and photos by HAL WAUGH

Reprinted from Alaska Sportsman®, July, 1960 (ALASKA® magazine)

"Look across the valley and count those snowslides starting from the right," I told Grancel Fitz. "When you reach the fourth slide you will notice it forks at the bottom."

"Gotcha!" was the reply.

"Follow along the skyline until you reach the steepest, most precipitous cliff."

"Gotcha!"

"Fine. Now draw an imaginary line from the base of that cliff to the left fork of that fourth snowslide. About halfway between is a bear."

After a few moments came Fitz's reply, "Gotcha again! But it would take a mountain climber to reach that bear!"

The mountain was steep and rugged, capped with a snowfield. Deep cuts, choked with snow, scarred its face, but as the season advanced each would become a small stream. A series of cliffs extended around the mountain, each offering dangerous climbing. To add to the difficulties, thick groves of alder were predominant with the only clearings being those scrubbed bare by snowslides.

In his present location, the bear was safe. All we could do was enjoy the sight of the huge animal and wish he would feed down our way.

We were looking for a trophy-sized bear from the "Lucky Knoll." When Grancel Fitz of New York and Boone and Crockett Club fame had first contacted me about a Kodiak Island bear hunt, his requirements were not unusual. He wanted a bear whose skull would score at least twenty-nine inches by Boone and Crockett Club standards. Translated into guide language, this twenty-nine-inch measurement called for a squared skin size of about ten feet.

The "Lucky Knoll" title resulted from the phenomenal good luck that had rewarded my clients and me with some outstanding trophies, spotted and stalked from this rocky, windy knoll.

From force of habit I turned to study a mountain behind us, that had produced some good trophies. Surprising me with his sudden appearance from nowhere, was a bear making his way downhill. He had a definite destination in mind, for he never slowed nor looked from left to right, but pushed with grace and power through the dense alders. Walking with unhurried strides, he soon moved beyond our sight without a chance for a shot.

"Oh my," Grancel groaned. "What I'd give for that one!"

Within minutes I'd located another bear. This one was on the skyline, making his way down a long ridge. From the first glimpse there was no doubt, trophy-wise, as to his value. Giving consideration to the fact that most skylined animals look large under certain atmospheric conditions, everything about this bear was just right—contour and general over-all appearance.

"Find the vee to the left of that rounded peak," I breathed, pointing.

Grancel mumbled in the affirmative.

"There's your bear. With a little luck we'll be going after him."

It was evident that my suppressed excitement was contagious. The bear was so good I had trouble holding my binoculars steady, and Grancel . . . his eye glasses bounced on his nose and his voice, when he finally found it, was stammering and unnatural.

Grancel Fitz looks over big bear country.

The rain had been falling steadily all day, and at this crucial time for us, the skies darkened and the precipitation, which had been just bearable, became a torrent. Visions of Grancel trying to sight through a big blurb of water on his 'scope lens tormented me as I led the way from the lucky knoll, across a muskeg flat toward the rolling foothills which we had to climb to get in shooting position.

Grancel was in good physical condition and made good progress through the wet grass and tangles of willow and alder. Yet, it seemed that any tortoise could have defeated us in a race, so great was my desire to get within shooting range of this exceptional trophy.

3

After ages we reached the top of the hill. I crawled like a snake through the final obstruction of brush to get my first close-hand look at our bear. He was ambling in our direction toward a small pothole. The massive head convinced me quickly, and I whispered to Grancel, "Take him!"

My binoculars afforded one of the most exciting views a hunter could witness. I waited for the shot. The bear was unaware that danger was threatening, but was displaying a marked tendency to work to his left toward a maze of alders. An imperfect shot would allow him to bolt into the alders and possibly be lost. It would be a dangerous bit of work at best, to dig him out of such a thicket if he ever got to it wounded.

Tearing my eyes away from the binoculars I turned to see just why Grancel hadn't complied with my demand to "Take him." I stared aghast. There was Grancel hurriedly wiping the accumulated rain from the lens of his binoculars.

"You don't have to look at him through those. I've looked at him. Take him!" was my strangled exclamation.

Turning back to the bear, I waited, dying a thousand deaths, wondering what I'd done to deserve this. Here was the finest trophy bear I'd ever seen and the most experienced hunter for a client I'd ever had, and yet . . . not a shot. Fortunately for my peace of mind the great beast had altered his course and was walking directly to the pothole as if he intended to wade into it.

Again turning to look over my shoulder to check on Grancel, I was confronted with a sight which would have been extremely comical at any other time. Grancel was trying, with all of the concentration at his command, to wipe both his telescope lens and eye glasses simultaneously, with soggy lens tissue and handkerchief. The rain was pouring down in sheets and most of his efforts were wasted.

With Grancel finally in shooting position, I turned to watch the bear. Now what! He was in the pothole lying down. "Oh no . . . don't shoot him in the water," I uttered. The roar of the '06 told me I'd spoken too late. A slight head movement by the bear was the only indication that a shot had been fired. Thinking that Grancel had missed, I said, "Shoot again, for Pete's sake." Another blast and still no action from the big buster. Odd!

Still another trophy from the Lucky Knoll nearly hides Waugh's Kodiak Island cabin. Big browns will square more than ten feet.

Straining my eyes until the tears ran, binoculars shaking as if I had the ague, it finally dawned on me. "That bear is dead!"

Wonderingly, I led the way to the pothole. Grancel stopped me with "Let me shoot him again." The comedy was still playing. Grancel mistook a hummock of grass about six feet in front of the downed bruin for his target and poured a shot into that. So identical in color was the bear to the weathered grass, so perfect the camouflage, that a casual glance would not have disclosed the bear's presence.

5

Contrary to my advice, Grancel had aimed for the neck. An instantaneous kill resulted. Earlier he had questioned me about the advisability of a neck shot. I promptly vetoed the suggestion, explaining that the target area was too small and too difficult. My advice was "keep 'em in the shoulders and boiler room." This good advice I will continue to pass on, regardless of the magnificent trophy then at our feet. The 145-pace shot was not excessive range, but it's about twice the range I prefer for shots at bear.

"I'm sorry I shot him in the water Hal, but my 'scope would have blinded out again with rain had I waited longer."

Neither Grancel nor I was particularly impressed with our first examination of the bear half submerged in water as he was. When I waded out and tried to lift the massive head, we began to revise our opinion. His muzzle had dropped at the shot and was buried in the soft, mucky bottom of the pothole. We were faced with back-breaking labor to get this bulky Kodiak out of the water to a position where the skin could be removed.

As we took rough measurements and made calculations our enthusiasm mounted. This was the bear we were after. No doubt about it. Let it rain, and who cared about the awkward position our bear had fallen in? I would hike out to get Jim Woodworth and Park Munsey, who were cutting firewood on the beach, to help us.

The only thing that really mattered was the fact we were quite positive we had a winner which had been killed humanely and quickly. It was the quickest bear kill I had ever witnessed.

Leaving Grancel to expose what pictures he wanted, I took off to get my other men. Fortunately I hadn't far to go, for they had heard the shooting and were making their way to our location.

"Did you get him? How big is he?" was their greeting.

In my excitement, all I could reply was, "He's big . . . boy, he's big!"

Back at the bear kill we lifted and tugged, tried several types of jury rigs, tied nylon line to alders and pulled on them. After herculean efforts, the big bear was halfway rolled and tugged on the bank where we could skin him. We therewith decided to leave the skinning for the next day and headed for camp.

That evening we guessed at his skull measurements and talked out the award possibilities, for Grancel would surely win an award with this bear. And, he did. It took first in the 1956 Boone and Crockett Club competition. All agreed that the "Lucky Knoll" was still producing, that I'd probably made it five in a row—five clients in that many years with bear for the record book.

Grancel surely established some kind of record for North American sportsmen, having hunted all classes of North American big game. Today's success should run the count up to thirteen record class heads. Little wonder we were a prideful lot that evening.

The next day, disregarding the downpour, we removed the big bear's skin and head, taking various measurements as we progressed. The neck measured 45½ inches in circumference just back of the head after the skin was removed. Lying on his side, the big fellow measured 57 inches from the top of his shoulder to mid-pad on the foreleg, giving an estimate of his height. The front pad measured 9 inches across and the rear pad was 13¾ inches in length. The longest claw was a full 6 inches long. The squared hide size was an honest 10 feet, 3½ inches. We estimated the green hide made a 160-pound pack, though Jim, Park and I would have sworn it was heavier, as we took turns lugging it to the beach and the dory.

After Grancel's hunt, Doctor Robert Rausch, Arctic Health Center and United States Department of Health representative of Anchorage, Alaska, spent two weeks at my Deadman's Bay camp making scientific observations. With his findings I feel freer to give an estimate as to a bear's possible weight, for Doctor Rausch weighed several Kodiak bear piecemeal, cutting up the carcasses and weighing chunk by chunk.

Too the world's record brown or Kodiak bear killed by Roy Lindsley on Kodiak Island in 1952, weighed 1190 pounds in the spring, shortly after emerging from hibernation. Thus it follows that Grancel's bear would also have weighed an approximate 1150-1200 pounds. By fall it might have gained two or three hundred pounds.

The skull of Grancel's Kodiak bear scored 30 5/16 after the waiting, or drying, period or sixty days. This was the same measurement we had determined at my Deadman's Bay cabin with the use of homemade calipers.

The Lucky Knoll had come through again.   ■

Dalls From
The Glacier Country

Charles Keim

*The author (standing) and Wayne look over the glacier-hung crests of
the Mt. Wrangell area and some fine sheep country.*

By CHARLES J. KEIM

Reprinted from Alaska Sportsman® , May, 1961 (ALASKA® magazine)

Wayne Matley, a Nevada cattle rancher from Reno, raised his head once more above the tiny ridge that hid us from the three Dall sheep rams. He peered intently through the binoculars at the snow white animals approximately 175 yards away. "Dammit anyway!" he muttered as he lowered his glasses, then rested his arm. "I don't know, Chuck."

I looked at Fred Boyle, cocked my fingers like a pistol, pointed them in the direction of the sheep and shook my head, knowing that Wayne couldn't see me. All three rams were more than three-quarter curl legal ones, but I thought we could do better. Fred did too, because he nodded in agreement, then continued to look over the huge valley and the surrounding peaks. That's Fred—always hunting, whether standing, sitting, lying down or walking.

"You make the choice, Wayne," I said. "They're all nice sheep. We might be able to do better."

Wayne started to look at me then shifted his gaze to where Fred was pointing far, far up the valley, almost to the knife-edge ridge that separated us from one of the major glaciers in the Wrangell mountains of south central Alaska.

"Two rams, Chuck," Fred said. "They're big and they're going to cross that snowdrift."

We all shifted our binoculars to the snowdrift. Sure enough, they were big rams, bigger than the three I kept sneaking quick looks at in case they should decide to quit feeding on the lichens and alpine grasses and head out of gunshot range.

"Well, we're into the sheep, even if it did take us some real work to find them," I said. "Should we give up these three and try for the two?"

Fred nodded affirmatively, all the while keeping his glasses on the pair he'd spotted. Wayne rolled over on his side and reached deep into his pocket for his plug of tobacco. He bit off a big chew, rolled it into his jaw and hazarded another peek over the ridge at the three animals, then said, "Let's go, even if we miss those others and have to do some more siwashing."

10

That's exactly what we'd been doing for six days, ever since bush pilot Jack Wilson had dropped our clients into our base camp near mighty Mt. Wrangell. I'd completed my summer teaching schedule at the University of Alaska where I was head of the journalism and creative writing department and now am dean of the College of Arts and Letters. Now I was working as a registered guide for Hal Waugh, Alaskan guide and outfitter. Fred was my assistant guide. He was head of the University's physical education department and now is president of a college in the State of Oregon. Three other persons departed from base camp with us and planned to hunt a nearby area. They were Guide Dale Miller, teacher at Valdez; Dr. Arthur Wills, associate professor of philosophy and English at the University, now helping out as packer, and Dr. Nick Klaich, who was Dale's client and a Reno friend of Wayne's. Nick wanted a sheep, too, and eventually got one.

We were in rather inaccessible country. Hal had scouted the area from the air for five years to find a place he thought the plane could use. Then he'd hired a trapper to pack in and clear off some of the rocks and brush, and we'd all worked on the strip the previous year to make it safe.

A guide always wonders a little about the kind of clients he's going to get, but any doubts we had on that score were immediately erased when Jack flew in Nick and Wayne in separate trips with his Supercub.

Both of our hunters had insisted on packing some of their gear as we prepared to head out for spike camp, approximately four miles up the valley. They were enthusiastic about the 46 sheep we'd spotted on the high peaks and, most of all, were experienced hunters who loved the outdoors, too.

"I don't necessarily want a Dall that will go in the Boone and Crockett Club's **Records of North American Big Game**," Wayne said as we trudged along the noisy, glacier-fed stream that tumbled down the canyon. "I'll be quite content if I get a trophy with well balanced horns, and I'd even like for them to be a little broomed at the tips. Seems to me something I should see on North America's top game trophy."

Wayne is after the Grand Slam in the sports world. The fore-end of his well used .270 rifle stock had a string of approximately 20 notches cut into it, all attesting to the fact that he likes to hunt and eat venison. He'd carved a big X for the desert sheep he'd bagged in Nevada. He was hoping this trip to add another X for the Dall. Later on he'd try for two more X's: a bighorn and a Stone.

We pitched our light mountain tents near a riotous clear stream, made a stew from the meat Hal thoughtfully had flown in, then, tired from our hike, we crawled into our sleeping bags. That night the cold crept down from the nearby glaciers and froze tiny chimes of ice which the water played for us before the sun rose.

Dall season opened that morning and we fully expected to see some of the sheep which we'd spotted from our base camp. But each white spot we examined with our glasses and the spotting 'scope proved to be either a rock or a patch of old snow which successfully had resisted the best efforts of the summer sun.

We powwowed then and finally decided that we'd hike upriver, skirting the massive ridge on which we'd seen some of the sheep from base camp. If necessary, we'd climb the ridge and hunt above the numerous canyons which fingered from it.

The first day proved two things to the three of us. We were in fair physical shape, and the sheep had moved out.

We headed back to spike camp, stopping occasionally to regain our breath, roll a cigarette and read the stories other inhabitants of the

Dall rams.

Charles Ott

river canyon had written in the small, sandy beaches which the fluctuating glacial stream soon would erase.

Here a ground squirrel had scampered along the bank, his tiny tracks punctuating the heavy messages left by a grizzly and her cub. A moose had meandered up and down the bank, determinedly had plunged into the water and resumed implanting his prints downriver on the opposite bank. And about the time we'd left the campus for the hunt, a band of sheep had walked almost single file higher along the water, then scrambled up the bank to the tundra which had blotted up their prints. Our vision for these messages had become a bit blurred since the previous fall's hunt, but we were content. Soon we'd almost be able to see even the quarry of the eagle which floated and aimed on motionless wings high above us, rocketed downward then ricocheted back into the blue clutching his trophy in his talons.

"Well, I guess it's Old Man Canyon tomorrow," Fred said. I nodded in agreement as I took my turn at the frying pan and kettles in spike camp. Over another cup of tea and my pipe, I explained to Wayne that Hal's client and Wayne's friend, Dr. Bob Broadbent of Reno, had named the canyon the previous year when he'd gotten a big ram there after a rather arduous climb. And Bob is an energetic young man.

We placed a lunch, ponchos, rope, and 'scope and a few "extras" in our packs and tied our shoepacs on our pack frames. Then in our hip boots we sloshed up the clear creek which narrowed and deepened as we approached the canyon it had cut from the solid rock hill.

Right—Wayne put sheep liver in the pan the next morning.
Charles Keim

13

Soon each man was left to his own thoughts as the water roared at its confinement and challenged us to find a route that wasn't deeper than our boots. Finally the creek widened, so we crossed to the other bank.

"What a place this would be to plant some trout," Fred said as we hung our boots high in a tree and laced on our shoepacs.

"You mean what I'd give for about half of this water in Nevada," Wayne laughed after we had drunk our fill. He reached into his pocket and solemnly handed his tobacco to Fred and then to me. We hadn't "chawed" for a long time, but had we declined the proffered plug we'd have broken that understanding that quickly develops between men who love the hills. We'd work out as a team.

The creek continued to widen, funnel-like, until we reached the mouth of Old Man Canyon. We cautiously glassed the ridges on both sides and then climbed up the one on the right. For a long time we sat just below the top and expectantly looked over the miles of alpine meadows which sloped downward from the bases of jagged and cloudy peaks.

"Not a sheep," Wayne said at length. "They must be around somewhere. Why, we even saw them on that meadow from base camp."

He pointed to a long, sloping meadow which from base camp, far below, had somewhat resembled the front sight ramp of a rifle when viewed from the notch of the creek we'd just come up.

Again we all used our binoculars for a long time, systematically eliminating the "possibilities" with the 30-power 'scope. Then we examined each peak as the clouds would permit.

"They've evidently moved over the peaks at the head of the basin or those at the right," Fred said. "If they'd gone over the peaks at the left we'd have seen them when we hunted up the river canyon."

Fred evidently was correct. When we had observed the sheep from base camp for three days before Wayne and Nick arrived, we had noticed that the sheep would disappear from time to time. We had thought then that the animals were just moving up the canyon and out of our view.

We returned to spike camp, and Fred and Wayne went back up Old Man Canyon next day, hoping that the animals might have moved back in. Wayne and I did the same on the fourth day. The only sheep we saw was a band of 17, three drainages and five miles away. That night we all agreed that, like it or not, we'd have to start packing our camp on our backs.

We had located a sheep trail that angled up the rubbly steep end of the canyon closest to the creek. Early on the fifth day of the hunt we again walked up the creek canyon then, after fruitlessly scanning Old Man Canyon, commenced our slow hike up the trail. We spaced ourselves far enough apart that if the lead or second man should dislodge any of the rocks, there would be ample time for the others to scramble off and above the trail to avoid them.

We reached the top about noon and rested for a time, despite a heavy wind that whipped a light rain almost horizontally from the dense clouds which scudded across the peaks and through the wide valley far below.

"Well, we can't follow the ridges; they're just too steep and sharp," I said. Reluctantly we angled down the slopes of the new valley. When the storm ceased and the clouds lifted we could see that it was fully as wide as Old Man Canyon. Ages ago a now dead glacier had rumbled downward, scouring the canyon into a wide U shape. On the far side numerous waterfalls feathered hundreds of feet from the almost flat benches, beyond which were snow-covered summits. A silt-laden stream which snaked back and forth across the valley floor had deposited rocks and earth and leveled out the moraines to accommodate a heavy growth of scrub willows and other vegetation.

"Well, we'll name this Grizzly Flats," Fred said. "There's a beauty."

Through our binoculars we could see a huge grizzly bear slowly waddling through the brush and stopping occasionally to feed on berries. Then almost as though the bear sensed that he had an audience, he sat down and scratched his chest and fat belly. Next he awkwardly rolled over and began to play with a large moose antler.

"What a bear," Wayne said somewhat wistfully. "Wonder if we'll see one like that when season opens September 1?"

15

"You'll probably get a grizzly, but right now we've got to find those sheep," Fred replied.

"We've got grub for two days, plus our emergency dehydrated food," I said, so we decided to pick our way cautiously across the slopes and toward the valley on the other side of the far end of Old Man Canyon.

Darkness came early where we worked in the shadows of the high ridges. We built a fire from the whitened roots and limbs of scrub willow which had given up the fight for survival amidst the rocks. Then we unrolled our sleeping bags on a narrow band of moss which had crept out between two huge mounds of talus. Immediately after eating we crawled into the bags and planned the next day's hunt. We decided to ascend the ridge at the far end of Old Man Canyon and glass the valley below it.

"If the sheep aren't there, we're really going to have to do some searching, because in the next valley we'd be looking on the slopes of Mt. Wrangell itself," Fred said. Then he remained silent. Wayne and I talked for a while longer. When he began to answer me with incomprehensible mumbles, I kept my thoughts to myself. Then I, too, fell asleep, wondering whether the sounds of the waterfalls which the night breeze occasionally brought our way had ever before reached human ears. There was a certain pleasure in guessing that they had not.

By 10 o'clock the next morning we had climbed the high ridge at the end of Old Man Canyon and were looking down on a massive Y-shaped glacier, formed by the blending of two coming from separate canyons. For a full half hour we glassed the peaks, benches and valley. Finally Wayne saw approximately thirty sheep feeding in a tiny meadow entirely surrounded by snow and ice. But it would take us a full day to reach them, and at least two days to return to spike camp from there.

"I'm reluctant to try to stretch our grub that long," I told Wayne while Fred climbed a needle-like peak approximately 1,000 yards away to peer down into the head of the last gulch that lay between our position and Mt. Wrangell. I hated to voice what I knew we were both thinking. We would have to return to spike camp and either get more grub so we could try for the sheep we'd just seen, or head out after the sheep we'd spotted on the fourth day of the hunt.

"Well, let's wait until 'Ol Scout' reports," I said to Wayne. "He's got something on his mind."

Fred had descended the peak and now was hurrying toward us, holding his rifle in front of him with both hands and jumping from rock to rock with the same nimbleness and grace that makes him one of Alaska's top skiers.

"I quit counting when I hit forty," Fred said as he sat down to regain his wind. "They're in that gulch. Lots of them. I couldn't see the entire gulch from where I was standing. But they're there."

We spent another two hours working below Fred's lookout point, then we belly crawled to the top of the ridge.

"Look at the sheep!" Wayne exclaimed.

We looked and counted. There were 110 of them, at first glance seemingly mostly ewes and lambs, feeding, resting and playing on the floor and sides of the gulch. It was approximately a mile and a half long and resembled a huge, slightly curved fan, split down the middle by the rocky bed of a creek and gently spreading outward and sloping upward to a long ridge.

"I'm darned if you don't look like a Nevada sheepherder looking over his flock," I told Wayne as we began to look for the rams which often like to remain somewhat apart from the band. We located many of them, but all appeared to be half or less curl.

Finally at the lower end of the gulch we located three sheep that were at least three-quarter curl and maybe more. We decided to pick our way downward, screened by the ridge, and then work up the creek bed toward the three animals. There was no way we could work from the head of the gulch without being seen.

When we reached the lower end of the gulch we stripped off our packs and prepared to stalk. We worked through a miniature Grand Canyon at the end of the gulch. Wind and water had carved tiny spires, mesas, pyramids, and domes from the soft rock. None of the formations was more than thirty feet high. Perhaps later on we'd be able to admire this multi-colored handiwork of Nature, but now we had sheep foremost on our minds.

We hugged the creek bank and were thankful for the noisy way the water tumbled downward, and that the breeze was blowing the same direction. When we were close to where we thought the three rams would be, I crawled up the bank. First I saw two, then three and finally seven ewes and lambs. I slid back down out of their sight.

"These sheep aren't spooky, and we're lucky about that," I told Fred and Wayne. "We're going to have to risk being seen by the ewes and lambs because if we wait much longer those rams are apt to move out. I'll crawl back up to that mound. It should put me in range of the rams. If they're still there, I'll signal."

I crawled then, in full view of the seven ewes and lambs. They watched curiously, then again began to feed. One ewe stamped her hooves a few times, then joined the others.

I took off my hat and slowly raised on my arms.

Charles Keim

Wayne looks over his Dall trophy while Keim's assistant guide Fred Boyle sizes it up for a packing job.

The rams were approximately 175 yards away, continually feeding, then looking about. Slowly I lowered myself and motioned for Fred and Wayne to join me.

"They're all well over three-quarter curl and the one on the left is the largest, but he won't make the book," I told Wayne. He looked them over, and that's when Fred noticed the two rams crossing the snowdrift at the head of the gulch.

We carefully crabbed backward, down the mound and into the creek bed to the nervous stamping of the alert ewe. Then we piled all our extra gear atop our packs and began moving upward. The first three-quarters of a mile was easy going. We stayed close to the creek bank, moving back and forth from the left to the right bank whenever

18

one appeared higher than the other. We could see ewes and lambs on both sides of us. They would give us a few curious stares, then resume feeding.

"I've seen domestic sheep wilder than these," Wayne said during a breather.

"Well, we aren't going to push our luck this last quarter of a mile," I replied. "This creek Y's out up there a ways and since the two streams will be smaller, we won't have the noise of the water to cover our movements. Then, too, both creek beds are shallower. Fred spotted the two rams so he'll accompany you on the final stalk. I'll tag along behind. There'll be less noise that way."

I wanted to stay up front, too, but I knew that my decision was a wise one. I remained about thirty-five yards behind the two men as they carefully picked their way over the loose rocks. Then Fred motioned to crouch, and after a time I could understand why.

Another ram had joined the pair. All three of the full curls were slowly feeding parallel to the rim which marked the terminus or, more accurately, the point of origin of the creek. And they were approximately 350 yards from the rim, beyond which there was absolutely no cover. The ridge of the mountain was another 350 or so yards behind them.

"It will be a long, uphill shot," I groaned to myself. Then I was comforted by the knowledge that Wayne's .270 had a 'scope and that long string of notches. I sat down and put my binoculars on the rams while Wayne and Fred slowly crawled up to the rim.

The rams were feeding, but ambling along after each nibble at the browse. Wayne would have to shoot fast or they would soon be so far to his left that he would have to pull another difficult and rapid stalk or risk a very poor side shot.

Wayne rested his rifle on the edge of the rim. Fred was lying alongside him. I watched Wayne dig deep into his pocket for his plug of tobacco. He clamped his teeth down on it, worried it for a moment then bit through. He deliberately shoved the plug back into his pocket, sighted for a moment then let go.

Two of the rams began running broadside to the left as the rifle shot echoed back and forth in the gulch. For a moment I couldn't see the third animal. Then I noticed that he was running in the opposite direction. I put my glasses on the two, expecting to see a crimson patch on the white hide. They stopped and looked back toward the third animal. He was gone.

"Down, I hope," I said to myself. There was no other explanation. Wayne surely would have dropped one of the pair that continued to look backward.

Fred stood up and raced forward a few yards.

"He's down!" he triumphantly shouted and the pair of rams started running. Wayne spat, let out a Nevada war whoop and ran uphill to his sheep.

"You beauty," he whooped, and to my astonishment kissed the big ram's rugged nose. I paced off the distance as I approached the kill.

"About three hundred and twenty-six yards," I said. "Taking a ram that might make the book with one shot at that distance entitles you to another kiss, I guess." I accepted Wayne's proffered plug; so did Fred.

We worked fast then to clean out the sheep, for darkness was beginning to fall, and a strong, cold wind had begun howling off the peaks. We still had to go down for our packs. It would be easier to cut over the ridge and go down the other side to the head of Old Man Canyon and follow it to spike camp than to retrace our steps made over the past two days.

"I'll cape him out in spike camp tomorrow," I told Wayne. "Since our grub is pretty low, we'll have liver for breakfast." We wouldn't be eating the heart. Wayne's shot had demolished it.

The wind was too cold and strong for us to bring our dehydrated soup and tea to a boil on the primus stove. We drank it lukewarm, then placed the meat and head twenty yards below us and covered it loosely with a sheet of plastic. The wind raged about us that night and whipped sudden flurries of snow from the low, black clouds. Fortunately, they were gone by dawn.

We broke through the creek ice with a rock to obtain water for washing and coffee. While we ate the sheep liver we looked about for the animals we'd walked through the previous day. Most of them were gone. A few ewes and lambs still fed on the lower slopes. We saw several more as we heavily ascended the ridge, laden now with the trophy and meat as well as our gear.

"I'm naming this place Siwash Meadows," Fred said as we took one last look before starting our descent into Old Man Canyon. "I'll bet there are sheep from here to Grizzly Flats."

We saw a number of good rams on our way back, but now the sheep hunt was over. Wayne got his grizzly a week later. He still claims that hunting the Dall provided his greatest challenge in Alaska. And he wasn't disappointed when the still green horns missed the book by a single point.

"I wanted those brooms at the end of each horn," Wayne said as he carved a big X alongside the other on the fore-end of his rifle stock. "Got to leave room for the bighorn and the Stone," he added with a grin. Both Fred and I sincerely told him we were sorry that we wouldn't be able to help him finish his Grand Slam. He'd proved to be the right kind of partner up there in the glacier country. ■

Big Trophies

Alaska has innumerable small lakes, most of them loaded with lake trout but protected on all sides by miles and miles of a miserable barrier—soft, squashy, sucking muskeg.

Story and photos by HAL WAUGH

Reprinted from Alaska Sportsman ®, April, 1958 (ALASKA® magazine)

We had finished our mixed-bag hunt in the Rainy Pass area of the Alaska Range. Sam Atkinson, my client, from McLeansboro, Illinois, looked at me with a big grin. "Hal," he said, "let's do some more hunting."

Though it was unplanned and unscheduled, I was agreeable. The date was September 12, 1955, and we had just completed a most successful hunt. Sam had secured a Dall sheep, a grizzly bear and a Stone caribou. Most sportsmen would have been ready to head for home, but Sam, eyes still red from the smoke of many campfires, still had the hunting urge.

23

Cow moose with calves would hurry off, but a lone cow was interested in our progress.

This was not my first hunt with Sam. In 1953 he had taken the best bear of the year from my Kodiak Island camp—a fine bear that scored 29-15/16 points and was awarded third prize in the 1954 Boone and Crockett Club competition.

Our spur of the moment decision made, we asked our pilot, Ward Gay of Anchorage, to fly us into south central Alaska where the moose are big and plentiful and where Sam could take another caribou if we should spot a good trophy. Relying upon Ward's recommendation for the exact location of our new camp, we flew with him the next day from Anchorage to Lake Louise in Ward's Grumman Widgeon and transferred to Cessna 180's for the final hop from Lake Louise.

A nice bull moose was on hand to greet our arrival at a small unnamed lake on the southern slopes of the Alaska Range. We looked him over carefully. He would have scored rather high, but we passed him up and enjoyed watching his unhurried retreat around the hillside above the lake.

Quickly we set up camp, then put on packboards and started on an exploration and game survey of this beautiful hunting country. Five bull moose and three bull caribou showed themselves that afternoon. We passed them up. We were after something outstanding, and hopes for an award winner were always in our thoughts.

The weather had turned cold and a brisk wind was blowing across the small lake, so the usual campfire chats after dinner were dispensed with. We were in bed soon after six in the evening. Sam occupied one of the small waterproof mountain tents. Larry Keeler, my packer, and I used a second one. A nylon tarp set up as a lean-to between the tents sheltered food and equipment.

On September 14 we made an early start, with Larry and me wearing the usual packboards, carrying lunches and camera gear. The nearby area proved to be some of the most photogenic country anyone could hope for. The foliage had turned to brilliant fall colors. We agreed that a trip into this lake for color slides and just plain lookin' would be worth anyone's time.

The cold would not permit comfortable glassing of the countryside for long periods, so we kept moving, stopping occasionally to look over some especially interesting spot. In this manner we located several moose and caribou, and we made approaches on two of the moose and one caribou to determine their trophy values. But the moose appeared to have no better than a 54-inch spread and the caribou was little better than mediocre. We called it a day and returned to camp for an early dinner.

The morning of the 15th dawned bright and clear, and though still cold, the day gave promise of excellent hunting. We chose a big valley extending miles to the west, with a gradual rise to a high plateau country that I knew was the home of several thousand caribou.

It was easy traveling up the valley. Some of the game trails were laid out as well as an engineer could have done it with technical equipment and a crew of men. When we had traveled about a mile we saw a lone Dall ewe come from the mountains to the north and cross the valley in front of us, evidently heading for the mountains on the south side.

We watched and worried for her until she reached the foothills, for on the lower levels, with brush to hide predators, a sheep's chances for survival are not so good as in their own high country.

We spotted several caribou, usually singletons. One cow moose with her calf hurried out of our way to hide behind a lone willow bush, leaving moose protruding from all sides. Surprisingly, a single bush or small tree can so well camouflage a moose that many hunters will not see it, even when studying a hillside carefully through binoculars.

By 10 o'clock I had spotted a small band of caribou with two medium-sized bulls sparring and trying out their newly polished antlers. Feeling that the canyon behind this band might offer us a suitable trophy, we made the climb for a better look. The gradual rise was not tiring. We managed to get into a good position on a small cliff overlooking the bedding ground of fourteen caribou. The animals were unsuspecting, and as we watched them from a distance of about 40 yards, they chewed their cuds, scratched and dozed. As nothing in the herd exceeded the bull Sam had taken on the earlier hunt, we withdrew quietly, unseen.

Descending to the valley floor, we carefully glassed the valley and hillsides. Later I learned that each of us was hoping to spot a wolf. We had walked past two separate wolf kills on the way up, and were now wolf conscious. No true sportsman begrudges the wolf the occasional

Sam used one small tent, Larry and I a second, and a tarp lean-to sheltered equipment and food. A brisk wind drove us to bed after dinner without the usual campfire chats.

Hal with trophies at Post Lake cache.

caribou, as this is nature's plan, but few hunters would pass up the opportunity to shoot at such a wily and intelligent animal. The wolf is a trophy to be proud of, and a skin mounted as a rug makes a most attractive wall hanging.

From our position we located three separate caribou bulls on the opposite side of the valley, and decided to make a try for the best one. The hillside was not very steep, but it was necessary to cross a big slide covered with barrel size rocks. Sam didn't enjoy this particular crossing, as great care was required to keep the rocks from cracking together and spooking the caribou.

Once across the slide, we had good cover and managed to sneak downhill to a point within 175 yards of the feeding bull. It was an easy shot for Sam, with his 'scope-sighted .270, and the 150-grain Cork-Lokt bullet shattered the spinal column at the neck for an instant kill.

Though it was not in the record class, I had given Sam the go-ahead signal on this caribou because it had the double shovels prized by hunters; a developed shovel protruded from the base of each antler, rather than a shovel on one side and a single tine on the opposing side. It has been estimated that the double shovel occurs once in five thousand caribou bulls.

With threatening weather to consider and a strong determination to bag a real trophy-size moose, Larry and I elected to pack the cape, antlers and meat back to camp in one trip. It was a decision which, after a short distance, we regretted with each step. Anyone who has packed a load on his back knows that any pack seems to have doubled its weight by the time you get it to camp. Our caribou was big, fat and heavy.

We were too tired to care about anything when we finally stumbled into camp. I'm afraid I set out a rather plain and hurried meal that night, as I'm positive I heard Sam mumble something to the effect that "Florence never served me anything like this back in McLeansboro, Illinois!" But I was too tired to care.

Next morning we were well rested and full of enthusiasm, and after breakfast the three of us set out for an interesting ridge to the east of camp. One small bull and another cow moose with a calf showed up, and in the distance below and across the flats and muskeg to the east, we counted seven moose feeding among the many small lakes. We were at timber line with firm terrain underfoot, and it would have required an exceptional moose, indeed, to tempt us to drop down into the soft, swampy, man-killing muskeg.

At noon, as previously planned, Larry returned to camp to flesh out the caribou cape. Fleshing is a tedious and time-consuming job, but a most important one to assure the hunter of a lasting and desirable trophy.

After our lunch of two sandwiches, cookies and a candy bar each, Sam and I continued around a ridge leading to the north and past the head of the lake. Though it has been my pleasure to view many a colorful fall scene in various parts of Alaska, I believe this south-central region is the most beautiful and appealing of all. Picture a wide valley, open to the south and guarded to the east, north and west by the rugged mountains of the Alaska Range. The bottom of the valley is studded with lakes—which, incidentally, are loaded in most instances with lake trout—but these lakes are protected on all

A moose will hide behind a single willow bush, leaving moose protruding from all sides. Surprisingly, a bush or small tree can camouflage a moose so well you may not see it.

sides by the most miserable barrier nature could devise. Muskeg. Miles and miles of soft, squashy, sucking muskeg. From the bottom of the valley the foothills rise in fairly easy slopes with benches at their tops. It is these benches we hunt, usually the higher the better.

Our walk was so pleasant that we sat down often and snapped pictures, or just looked and grinned at each other, thoroughly enjoying ourselves and the day.

Climbing a ridge that looked gamey, we got down to the serious business of locating a moose. Finally we spotted a big bull in a dense clump of alders. He was moving our way and entertaining himself by practicing feints and vicious jabs at the brush with his well-developed rack—in preparation for the coming rutting season. It was a sight to see. Simultaneously Sam and I spotted a lone wolf working his way swiftly down a line of alders toward the moose, but the wolf was alone and it was apparent that the bull was in no danger. In fact, with the big bull in the mood he was demonstrating, any single wolf would do well to steer its course in the opposite direction.

Sam's caribou was not in the record class, but it had the coveted double shovels which are found only once in five thousand bulls.

One brief glimpse of the wolf was all we got, and the moose remained in the same thicket. We agreed that the wolf was merely traveling in a line that took it in the general vicinity of the moose. The bull had a rack that would measure 55 or 56 inches. Feeling we should do better, we passed him by and made a leisurely loop that landed us in camp in time to prepare and consume a much more complete meal than the hurried snack of the night before. This night I heard nothing about the meals served in McLeansboro, Illinois, topped off with pecan pie.

Saturday, September 17, was bright and clear but still fairly cold. I determined to make a climb up the mountain to the south where we had been seeing moose. With the caribou cape well fleshed and salted and tied into a neat bundle, Larry was free to accompany us and give us the useful third pair of eyes.

During the climb we looked over two smallish bull moose and a caribou cow. The mountain was easy climbing, with big spots of open country and a few pot holes that showed by multitudes of tracks that they were used as watering holes.

We attained a knoll that offered good visibility, and while we were glassing, a small bull moose appeared. He was watching his backtrack and he seemed nervous. We didn't have long to wonder what was bothering him. A real buster of a moose came aggressively out of the brush and ran the smaller bull around the mountain, then returned to feed just above us and roughly 600 yards away. His actions showed clearly that he too was feeling the rutting instinct, just as the bull of the evening before. He would not condone any competition in his bailiwick.

It would have been difficult to make the uphill sneak without sufficient cover, and it was imperative that I get close to determine whether we were considering a first-class trophy with a good rack or just another big bull. Sam called me names but stayed right behind me, crawling along on his stomach as I did until we reached the protective cover of some willows. The light was never quite right, and it seemed that each time we moved a little closer there was a bit of brush or a small tree to obstruct our view.

Obviously this was a trophy to be proud of, but for a repeat client like Sam, so easy to guide and pleasant to be with, my mind was made up to take nothing less than a moose I was sure would place well up in the record book. Risky, but most exciting.

By now the big fellow had bedded down, but in such a position that by turning his head he could command a view over a large area below him, which included our line of approach.

Our good luck held. We finally reached a point from which we had a good view of the bull, and each time he turned his head I was more sure he was the one we wanted.

We were now at the critical time for the guide—a most exciting yet exasperating period. Once a bullet is fired and the animal hit, there is no turning back, and a guide's mistake in judgement can send the hunter home disillusioned with the guide's ability to judge a trophy.

As usual Sam didn't interfere or offer suggestions, but left the decision entirely up to me. That is what any wise, experienced hunter should do.

The moose is one of the most difficult of the Alaska big game animals to judge from a trophy standpoint, and it was with some misgivings that I said, "Better take him, Sam."

Although I cannot recommend the .270 Winchester for big bears or moose, in Sam's competent hands the .270 has accounted for eight

In Sam's competent hands the .270 Winchester has accounted for eight trophy animals out of Alaska. The bull moose shown above, Sam's fifth trophy of the year, had a 65 5/8 inch spread and scored 223 2/8 Boone and Crockett points for third place of the season.

Alaskan trophy animals. This big bull staggered around, but went down to be finished easily with a close-up neck shot, the fifth trophy for 1955.

We were three tense hunters as I put the tape to the antlers. Then a shout of elation from all. The tape showed a spread of 65 5/8 inches. The willingness to wait and pass over several bulls had paid off again, as Sam's moose was awarded third place in the 1954-55 season and will be found listed with the top 20 of the all-time records.

He was extremely fat, round as the proverbial butterball, and later my family and friends agreed that he was the best and tastiest moose we had yet eaten. It was fortunate that there were three of us to work with the dressing and skinning. Very soon we were to wish that we had a great deal more help in packing out the meat, antlers and cape. Our trip down the mountain, through a creek bottom, fording a swift mountain stream, up a steep bank and into camp, was something none of us will soon forget.

The rack alone, which I carried, weighed 91 pounds, and a more awkward pack would be hard to contrive. Strapped well down on my packboard, the antlers extended so high into the air that I was forced to attach a line to the tops and to hold the end of the line in my hand to offset the tendency of the pack to topple me backward. Every limb and twig caught on the antlers.

Larry, tremendous packer that he is, moved all the meat part way down the mountain to make a cache on top of some rocks and in addition made two complete round trips to camp with the cape and some meat. Again we were a tired trio in camp, with sore shoulders and aching muscles, but our satisfaction with the trophy at least partly offset the fatigue and we were most cheerful. For some reason, dinner that night tasted extra delicious—at least to me, the cook.

The next morning I started the slow fleshing operation while Sam and Larry went back after the rest of the meat. Not many hunters volunteer to help with this backbreaking job, but big, powerful Sam said, "I can't pack like you fellows, but I'll do what I can." The way that meat came down the mountain I'm sure both Larry and I thought we had a first-class packer with us.

Larry carried his rifle constantly, as we had no desire for bear trouble. It was on the way out that we learned an Anchorage resident had been killed by a grizzly not many miles from our camp, and during our hunt. Soon afterward, many miles to the south, on the Chilkat River north of Haines, a prominent Haines sportsman was to pay a terrible bill in pain and terror because he returned to the scene of his moose kill unarmed. He suffered the loss of three ribs and part of one finger and more than a hundred tooth marks, and survived.

When bears are involved, there are certain rules that must not be broken. We who hunt bears professionally have learned to put up with them, and always try to observe the rules. The sportsman, be he Alaskan or nonresident, will do well to stay completely away from the big bears unless he is accompanied by a professional guide or is well qualified in his own right through years of experience. And countless experiences with bears are required, not just those of an occasional hunt.

A good Alaska law requires that the meat from all trophy animals, bears excepted, be saved and utilized. In my camps, unless the hunter wishes to take the meat home (few do), we eat what we need and the remainder is distributed among the guides, packers and cook and, if occasion arises, to some needy family. To many of us the meat from the trophy animals killed in the fall constitutes a most important item in our year's food supply.

Big, powerful Sam Atkinson, easy to guide and pleasant to be with, preferred the meals back in McLeansboro, Illinois, but he certainly liked the hunting he found in Alaska.

As Larry and Sam progressed with the meat-packing, I was experiencing a most miserable fleshing job. It was cold and windy and my hands could scarcely hold the fleshing knife. By nightfall, however, I had completed the fleshing and with Larry's help had the cape salted and tied into a bundle. We were all so pleased to have the work done and the big moose rack to gloat over, that dinner and the evening were again most cheerful.

Ward was due to pick us up the next day—and by now we had a third trip planned for the season, a short hunt on the Kenai Peninsula for goat and black bear.

The next day one of Ward's planes flew over camp, so we reasoned that we would be picked up as scheduled. It can get rather nerve-racking, out in some remote spot waiting for an airplane to arrive. The weather may look fine in your locality, with unlimited visibility, high ceiling and no wind, yet common sense tells you that miles away, back at the hangar, the weather may be boiling and unfit for any flying. Also, out in the bush with no way of knowing what's going on in the world, after you've been stranded for a while you can get to wondering whether some disaster has overtaken civilization.

Our present concern was ice, which was forming around the shore of the lake and by next day could make it impossible for a float plane to land. We broke camp and made everything ready for a fast loading. At three in the afternoon we heard the welcome sound of an approaching motor. Soon Howard Smith, who flies for Ward, was greeting us from his Cessna 180.

As our lake was small it was necessary to ferry light loads out to a nearby larger lake, where the Cessna could take out a full load. This was accomplished in four trips, and my relief was great when the last load was in the air. I was the last man out, and while I waited for Howard I could imagine all sorts of trouble developing with the plane, and I wondered how uncomfortable I would be with a campfire and some barbecued meat.

But the return to Anchorage was uneventful, merely reversing the incoming procedure. Cessna 180's to Lake Louise and the Grumman Widgeon on to Anchorage. It had been a truly wonderful hunt, successful for both the guide and the guided. Sam and I are now planning his third Alaska hunting trip.   ■

Spooky Birds At Summit Lake

Summit Lake is in the frozen but beautiful Alaska Range.

By CHARLES J. KEIM

Reprinted from Alaska Sportsman®, May, 1956 (ALASKA® magazine)

"Git 'im boy, give 'im an uppercut!"

These were the first words that greeted us when we stopped at the Buffalo Lodge at Big Delta, Alaska, one April and asked the friendly owner, George Norton, how ptarmigan hunting was down the Richardson.

"Some hunters really have been getting them near Summit Lake and Paxson Lake," George said. Then my partner, Joe Fetzer, then head of the University of Alaska business administration department, asked George "how come" he was screening a movie of a boxing match.

George replied that a brewing company makes the films available, and the whole neighborhood had dropped into the lodge to see the

37

Hunting ptarmigan on snowshoes is a strenuous, but enjoyable sport, and these elusive birds are delicious to the taste.

fight which they had been anticipating for a long time. George runs his lodge like a home for a big family, and there is a big family in the neighborhood—hundreds of GI's from nearby Fort Greely.

The projectionist finished changing the reel, and Joe and I watched the last few rounds with interest. Meanwhile, George told us we should try the Summit Lake area first. If we didn't run into ptarmigan, we should go on to Paxson Lake. We already had driven approximately 100 miles southeast of Fairbanks, but if there were ptarmigan we didn't mind going another 80 or so.

We knew there were ptarmigan in the area. Bush pilots had reported seeing hundreds of the birds, which are about the size of a ruffed grouse, and which change their nondescript brown summer feathers to white ones in the winter. One pilot had told me that many miles away from the highway the sides of the hills literally were alive with the birds. Wildlife men generally agreed the ptarmigan seemed to be approaching a peak in their cycle.

"You'll get ptarmigan," George assured us as he poured our coffee. "The birds are a bit spooky, but you two 'profs' ought to be able to outsmart them. After all, Chuck, you're an old-timer at ptarmigan hunting."

That friendly dig drew a laugh all around. Two weekends before, I'd gotten away from my classes for another ptarmigan hunt. Jim Rearden, Alaska photographer-writer, and I had tried to get into the Paxson area.* A blizzard had forced us back. We had gotten one bird, the only one I had been able to get close enough to shoot.

Out of shotgun shells, I killed these birds with a K-22 revolver.

Now the highway that had stopped the hunt was open, a tiny, vital thread weaving through the cold but beautiful wilderness of the Alaska Range of mountains.

*Today, 18 years later, Rearden is Outdoors Editor for ALASKA® magazine.

Joe and I camped out that night near frozen, silent Summit Lake, sleeping warm in our down bags. The snow on both sides of the highway towered high above the car and protected us from the wind which moaned its protests at the intruders of its white domain. We made coffee with snow, and fried bacon and eggs over our little gasoline stove Saturday morning. Then we decided to head down to Paxson and hunt back toward Fairbanks.

Several ptarmigan flew across the highway after we passed Paxson Lodge. Another car was parked along the highway, indicating some hunters already had strapped on their snowshoes and headed into the willow and spruce. Soon we passed more cars and saw their GI occupants getting set for the hunt.

We drove another half-mile. Then we noticed ptarmigan tracks on the light blanket of snow that had fallen during the night. I belted on my K-22 revolver. Before we left the car, Joe agreed to pack the game bag which carried the extra shells until I got a ptarmigan. From then on the bag would change hands each time one of us got a ptarmigan.

We strapped on our snowshoes and headed across a flat valley intersected by the cold Gulkana River which had broken winter's grip and was tumbling deep and wide over ice-covered rocks. Behind the river the mountains rose white and steep. Two bull moose stopped breaking off willow branches, stared belligerently at us for a few moments then lumbered painstakingly away from us toward the river. They paused now and then to stare back at these creatures who were

Along the highway we passed a trapper's cabin and cache.

40

walking on the snow while they broke through the crust at each awesome lunge.

Several large flocks of ptarmigan whirred overhead, well beyond the range of Joe's single-barrel and my automatic 12-gauge. All of the birds headed across the river which we apparently couldn't cross. And they were acting just like those birds Jim Rearden and I had encountered two weeks before—spooky and not a bit interested in getting some higher education from a couple of university profs who were tossing out number eight shot instead of "book learning."

In the distance, toward the highway, Joe and I could hear other shotguns booming, indicating the GI's were flushing birds. Soon we heard more of the flocks above our heads and heading across the river.

"Well, all the birds are across the river," I gloomily told Joe. "I guess the best we can do is head back toward those willow clumps we skirted and see if we can jump a stray flock."

Joe conceded that this seemed the best plan. Then we encountered two sets of fresh moose tracks broken deep into the hard-crusted snow skirting the river bank. The moose, possibly those we had alerted, seemed to know where they were going. But they were having a tough time of it. Repeated breaking through the crust evidently had worn their legs raw, for we found a thin circle of blood near the top of most of the tracks.

We decided to follow the tracks, and our decision paid off. They led to an ice bridge. There was open water on both sides of the bridge, and an almost imperceptible fog silently rose into the ten degrees above zero air.

"It held moose—let's try it, Chuck," Joe said.

I snowshoed over, carefully watching for any indication that the bridge was weakening. Joe followed so I could get a picture of this convenient ice bridge being crossed. Both of us kept our eyes on a patch of willows where the last flock of ptarmigan had landed. There was no telling if they would be there when we arrived. Those birds can run over the snow like scared snowshoe hares.

We separated and cautiously approached the clump. Soon we head the "troonk, troonk" of the sentinel ptarmigan, indicating the birds were ready to flush. They sounded like giant frogs.

Whirrr!

Beautiful weather and plump ptarmigan made a good hunt.

About twelve ptarmigan took off to Joe's right. He swung his shotgun toward the lead bird as they accelerated to about the speed of an Hungarian partridge.

Joe's shotgun boomed. His first ptarmigan dropped. He held it triumphantly aloft. It was a willow ptarmigan whose beak is larger in proportion to the head than is that of the rock ptarmigan. Also the willow is a bit larger than the rock, and the rock, in winter coat, has a black line running from the beak through the eye. After we had examined Joe's ptarmigan we headed toward the flock which had flown part way up the mountain.

As we climbed we could hear other shotguns banging in the distance. Evidently the hunters on the other side of the river had encountered some birds, but from our vantage point on the slope we could see that we were the only ones across the water.

A flock of approximately 100 birds whirred high above our heads. We watched as they flew through the valley. They had shaken the men with guns, but another hunter was leisurely pacing them. It was a gyrfalcon following every twist and turn of the flock and maintaining the same distance between himself and his white prey. He was in no rush to strike, but Joe and I were sure that he'd be eating ptarmigan before we would.

When the flock was out of sight we agreed to split-up for a short time. I would hunt higher up the mountain and Joe would hunt below.

I had planned to transfer the shells from the hunting bag Joe was packing into my own pocket. But a ptarmigan broke from a clump of willows above me just as we decided to spread out. I headed for that bird and dropped it and two others which flushed at my first shot.

I reached into my pockets to reload and found exactly three shells. They would have to do me until I reached Joe.

Moose led us to an ice bridge across the Gulkana River.

It was tough snowshoeing up the steep hillside. I could hear the "troonk-troonks" all around me. I missed my first two shots at a ptarmigan that flushed ahead of me and streaked low up the mountain. He tumbled at my third shot which spooked fully 200 birds. The air seemed filled with the fleeting white balls—all out of shotgun range, but it made no difference. My shotgun was as useless as a club, and those birds weren't about to be club-hunted anyway. But I still had a K-22 revolver with six bullets in it.

The flock headed down the mountain far ahead of where I figured Joe would be. They finally settled on a small hill fairly close to the river. I hightailed it down the mountain, planning to head off Joe, get some shells, then together we could approach the flock.

43

.

I was in too big of a rush. One of my snowshoes slipped off a snow-covered lens of ice and I tumbled headlong into four feet of snow. My shoes crossed and there I was—unable to flounder to my feet and not exactly knowing which way was up. Finally I was able to roll a ways down the mountain until I reached a spruce tree. Grasping its branches, I slowly pulled myself erect, brushed the snow from my parka, emptied the stuff from my pockets and slowly went back to retrieve my shotgun.

This accident kept me from meeting Joe where I had planned. I didn't want to shout because I was afraid I would further spook the large flock of ptarmigan.

When I finally got behind the last spruce separating me from the flock, I could see approximately 200 ptarmigan. They were about 50 yards away, preening and fluffing their feathers in the 10 degrees above zero sun. I was warm from my exertions, but red hot mad at myself for not packing the extra shells for my shotgun. I peered around the spruce. All the ptarmigan we had seen that morning had been spooky. This flock now seemed quite the opposite, almost as if sensing they were safe from shotgun fire.

I had no compunctions about shooting at them with my K-22. I would do the same if they were rabbits at that distance, or much other small game.

Bang! A miss.

I shot again and dropped a bird. The others looked at it for a moment and then went back to their preening. I dropped two more before my bullets were gone.

Then there was nothing else I could do. I snowshoed up the hill with all the birds watching me, the sentinels' "troonks" growing louder with each step I took. When I was about 30 yards away they all took off with a whir that reminded me of a combine cutting a swath in a Montana wheat field.

Back at the car I gratefully gulped down a can of grapefruit juice. The snowshoeing up and down the mountain had dehydrated my body. Joe soon joined me. Our bag was 11 birds between us.

We settled down for the night, resolving that the next day we would hunt the area where I, with no shotgun shells, had watched the birds.

On Sunday these birds just forgot their good manners of the day before. They would fly away from us, settle, then run like the dickens. I finally quit trying to use the shotgun, and we succeeded in bagging five that morning. My longest shot with the K-22 was 64 yards. Joe, who had substituted his .22 repeater for the shotgun, dropped a couple from an even greater distance.

We earned those 16 birds. Then Joe and I decided to head back towards Fairbanks, even though we didn't have our full limit of 15 per day per hunter. Actually, we were entitled to 30 apiece for the weekend hunt.

When the birds flew across the river we almost lost them.

We had passed several other open streams on our way to the hunting area and thought we might be able to catch a few grayling to round out our trip. While we were strapping our snowshoes onto the car, we probably prevented a hunter from bagging much larger game than our birds. He almost shot his partner.

The popping of .22 rifles drew our attention to the drama which we watched unfold from about 400 yards. Two civilians had stopped their car behind us and had climbed a hill near the highway. Evidently that had driven some ptarmigan into the brush.

One of the hunters snowshoed ahead of the other, and over the chill, clear air we heard, "I'll scare 'em out of the brush, then you shoot 'em."

"OK, Mert."

Soon Mert was about 40 yards ahead of his partner. Evidently he had scared the birds into running into the open, for we heard him say, "OK, there they are; shoot 'em."

"Crouch down, Mert, so I won't hit you."

We watched Mert "crouch." He was directly in front of his partner. Maybe Mert's partner couldn't see him because of the brush and shallow depressions, but from our vantage point we could tell he could shoot Mert.

"I'm goina' shoot now, Mert, are you down?"

"Yeah, shoot 'em."

Mert's partner raised his rifle. He was aiming right for Mert.

"Mert," I shouted.

No answer.

"Mert."

"Yeah?"

"You're going to get shot. Your partner is aiming right at you." There was silence.

"Mert, you're going to get shot."

Mert hollered to his partner—loudly.

"Don't shoot. Don't shoot. C'mon up here with me."

Mert's partner said something we couldn't hear. Soon the men were together, and started popping away, slowly moving over the crown of the hill.

When we were a few miles past Summit Lake on the way back to Fairbanks, we waved to a hunter walking along the road. He waved back, then motioned for us to stop.

"You guys hunting ptarmigan?" he asked.

When we said "yes" he pointed to the expanse of flat land which was to our left. "I just got my limit there; you ought to give it a try."

We did and it paid off. The easy snowshoeing more than compensated for the fact that the hunter who had tipped us off had spooked the birds. They began to show up in twos and threes, running over the snow then breaking into flight. My shotgun boomed three times and I had three ptarmigan, dropping like any pheasant I've ever bagged. I hastily scooped them up, placing them along my snowshoe tracks so I could retrace my steps and find them.

A lone ptarmigan zoomed into the air almost out of range. I dropped him, then spent the next ten minutes looking for the bird. Finally I found it. As it tumbled, it had gone headlong into the snow, breaking through the crust until only a trace of the black in the tail

Joe was anxious to get this ptarmigan in the game bag.

feathers showed. Joe was having the same good hunting, and the same trouble locating his kills.

This slowed us down, but it paid off, too. The spooky birds had a chance to settle down as we looked for their less fortunate companions.

Joe headed off to my right. He flushed four ptarmigan, downed one, and the rest of the bunch headed my way. I waited until they were out of Joe's way and swinging to my left. I led the front bird and he plummeted into the snow as my 12-gauge roared. Joe was popping away to my right and I could see him scouting around looking for his kills. For my money this was more fun than lots of the time I've spent waiting behind a blind to pop away at ducks as they winged into range.

I headed for the remaining two of the four Joe had flushed, loading as I ran on the snowshoes. I dropped them with two shots and picked up some more until I was ready to drop myself from my exertions.

By now most of the birds had flown a considerable distance from us. We could have snowshoed to them, but we decided we had plenty of birds, it was getting late and we had classes the next morning.

We checked our count when we reached the car. They were all willow ptarmigan.

"Forty," the business administration professor said. Then he added, "Let's go home and eat some."

We did just that for the next two weeks.   ■

47

Two Hunters, Two Bears

It was a late spring and in Deadman's Bay, above, where we went to hunt the giant Kodiak bears, snow still lay low in the passes.

Story and photos by HAL WAUGH

Reprinted from Alaska Sportsman® , December, 1957 (ALASKA® magazine)

Pleasant comradeship prevailed. The large coffee pot was exuding fragrant, steamy odors. Eagerly anticipating the coming hunt, we were in complete agreement that our Kodiak Island cabin was the best place on the continent this night. My clients, Bud and Jim Piper of Sterling, Colorado, looked and talked like hunters. Both were

49

experienced, and they possessed that gay enthusiasm reserved for the young and healthy.

The weather had given my crew a depressed feeling during the pre-hunt work. Intermittent rains and constantly overcast skies had taken the fun out of wood-cutting, dory repairs and countless other chores necessary to put a hunting camp in readiness. Normally, this is a satisfying period. But now, with our hunters in camp, our spirits were responding to the cheerful optimism that fairly oozed from them. We were ready to start a two-week hunt for the trophy that is tops with most of us who have hunted all Alaska game animals—the Kodiak bear.

Each game animal has something special to offer the hunter. Sheep hunting is wonderful. Anyone with a soul is both thrilled and inspired when he climbs the pinnacles and peaks to enter the domain of the Dall sheep. The giant, majestic moose has much in his favor. Caribou, too, have an intangible something which attracts many an admiring sportsman. Goats, in most instances, require much hard work and anyone with goat-hunting experience must respect the calm, rugged strength of North America's best and most versatile mountaineer. With all due respect to the qualities which give each species its own special appeal, the big Brown bear is still in a class by himself.

Countless words have been written and thousands upon thousands of dollars have been expended by guides and outfitters in publications, folders and pamphlets, in an attempt to describe bear hunting. Yet it remains necessary for the individual to experience an actual hunt to appreciate the thrill, excitement and special appeal involved in the pursuit of the Kodiak bear. Then, too, most of us who work at guiding are forever noticing and discovering small things which force us to reverse or change our opinions about the great bears. Perhaps this is part of the process of growing up, or growing older.

Bud and Jim had broken one cardinal rule of Kodiak bear hunting—both had arrived in camp minus the all-important hip boots. One of the curses attendant upon bear hunting is the hot, uncomfortable, hip boots necessary for fording creeks time and again and for wading to and from the boats and skiffs on the tide flats. If there is a blistering word to call footwear that hip boots have not been called, it must be something in a foreign language. The poor boots, in their innocence, have caused irate hunters and guides to call down the wrath of the hunting gods upon them, and summon their forefathers to witness the injustice of having to wear them. Little devils pull your best wool socks down around your toes. Larger little devils pull your heel up where your calf belongs.

Yet, wading without hip boots is not the lesser of two devils. As a guide, and one who just naturally wears hip boots, I have found it necessary to carry piggy-back a hunter who weighed 228 pounds. The sight might have been comical to an observer, but to a poor long-geared guide, the humor was absent.

The next four days we spent hunting out from camp, first in one direction and then in another. We were all gradually toughening up and working into hunting condition. Although we saw six bears during this period, none appeared to be the size Bud was hoping for. Seeing game early in the hunt served a useful purpose, however, as it kept our enthusiasm at a high pitch. Locating bear trails in the snow on a early

Bud, Larry, Ken and Jim, left to right below, the brothers in borrowed hip boots, prepare to shove off for a day's hunt. A dory, slow but reliable, saves countless footsteps.

spring hunt affords pleasurable and informative material for conjectures and analysis. Some trails are made by bears emerging from winter dens high on the mountains. Others are formed by bears seemingly wandering without aim or objective. Some trails lie in long, graceful curves, while others appear to be intricate geometric designs. Of never-failing interest is the unmistakable evidence that big Kodiak bears negotiate steep cliffs and precipices usually considered the terrain of sheep and goats.

More surprises are in store for the hunter as he sees bears apparently living high on the mountains in what seems, from the lower reaches at least, a world of solid snow. Closer observation discloses brush protruding from the snow. This vegetation is the attraction for the bears. They scoop the snow aside and dig up the roots for some of the first food they take after the hibernation period.

On the fifth day, Bud, Jim, guide Kenneth Condit and I traveled down the bay by dory to one of our favorite lookouts. The bears and

Bud and Jim Piper of Sterling, Colorado, lifted the camp crew's spirits. Experienced hunters, they were possessed of that gay enthusiasm reserved for the young and healthy.

the weather had evidently teamed up to make the day's hunt miserable and unproductive. It was foggy and windy. Visibility was nil. This was a late spring, and snow still lay low in the passes. Our little pocket primus stove produced excellent coffee as we huddled in the lee of the rocks.

After several hours of fruitless watching and continued overcast, we decided to return to camp. The 22-foot dory bounced considerably on the way back. Mel Horner, our venerable old cook, had cheer ready for the weary hunters in the form of a hot, delicious meal and great pots of coffee. The fire in the cooking range warmed the cabin and dried various articles of clothing as we visited and exchanged hunting experiences.

Another two days passed in unproductive hunting, with the bears spotted not bears wanted. Then it happened. The four of us had taken up comfortable sitting positions above Horse Marine Lake. Each was using his binoculars in an effort to be the first to spot a bear. This time I was fortunate. Traveling across-wind about a mile away was a fine big one. At my suggestion, Ken and Jim shed all unnecessary clothing and started across the muskeg. As they made their way through willows and alder clumps in an attempt to intercept the bear, Bud and I watched eagerly as they made a speedy, faultless approach.

But our pleasure and excitement were all the good that came of their perfect stalk. Unaware of the enemy in his vicinity, the bear was following his wandering and feeding instincts away from danger. Kenneth wisely gave up the stalk and returned to our vantage point, hoping the bear would not be spooked out of the country.

The day progressed slowly, with each man using his binoculars almost constantly in an effort to locate a bear—any bear, but preferably the big fellow that had given us the slip. Our perseverance was rewarded by the sight of two bears. Both were far away and appeared to be small.

Spotting game is not easy. A few hunters quickly tire of this part of the hunt and leave the spotting entirely up to the guides and packers. Generally they offer one of several remarks that have become standard to us guides—"You know what you're looking for. I'll just sit back here and relax." Or, "I trust your eyesight."

To these hunters I make no complaints and offer no suggestions, but the fact remains that two pairs of eyes will eventually see more than two eyes. After some practice at spotting, one can work out a little game by plotting imaginary rectangles and working each one out in turn, each overlapping the preceding one. Play this game and few suspicious spots or moving objects will be missed. We take time out for lunch, then everyone takes a turn at catching 40 winks about midday, when few bears are moving.

By late afternoon the skies had cleared and we were warm and comfortable. As a foursome, we seemed to feel that today, April 30, was destined to be just another day of hunting. At length I gave the word to pack up and begin our trek to the beach for the 50-minute boat ride to the cabin. I raised my glasses for a final scanning of the mountain on the south. Kenneth made a last-minute check on the mountain to the north.

Kenneth is normally a calm, quiet man, and I could sense urgency in his voice when he said, "Boss, I see a bear!"

Packboard on my back, I turned to locate the object of Kenneth's intensity. One good look was enough. This was a bear we wanted! In all probability it was the one that had eluded Ken and Jim in the morning. After a few hurried instructions, Bud and I were away without coats, packboards or other non-essentials.

Panting and perspiring, we climbed the last ridge between us and the one on which we'd seen the bear. It had been hard, fast going from the lookout. I was relieved to note that Bud was in good condition and able to do his end of the job properly, now that the crucial moment was at hand. The air seemed still and humid as we peered silently about, concentrating with every nerve alert.

There he was, directly below us, a strikingly beautiful sight as he waded a small creek. Big and glossy, he swung rhythmically along, dripping water as he mounted the low creek bank. Quickly Bud got into a good shooting position, and as soon as the bear cleared a patch of alders the fireworks began. He fired and bear was down. He got up. Again Bud fired and again the bear was down. Up! Down! Bud was taking no chances on losing this trophy.

Cautiously we worked down the ridge, giving Bud a needed opportunity to calm his nerves and recover his breath. Suddenly the

On mountains that look from below like worlds of solid snow, bears scoop the snow aside and dig up roots for some of the first food they take after their winter-long hibernation.

bear sat up in the position of a dog begging for a bone. I called softly to Bud, but he was almost too slow. The bear had spotted me, and I knew that in a second it might be necessary for me to put in a stopping shot. But Bud emerged from the alder patch and applied the *coup de grace*. His past hunting experience and the many hours he had spent hand-loading and firing this particular .300 magnum paid off.

After watching the bear for movement and making sure that he was really dead, I climbed back to the top of the ridge we had but recently descended and signaled to our watchers, Jim and Ken. Success! In the fast-fading light I opened the lens of my Exakta wide and took numerous pictures of the dead bear and the jubilant hunter while we waited for Jim and Ken to join us.

The bear was huge. Though I frown upon the hunter or guide who quotes irrelevant and possibly unreliable information about the size of a trophy, I will give a few of the measurements I took of this bear for my personal information. The rear pad was 14½ inches from the extreme back of the pad to the tip of the longest claw. I have measured few pads that were longer. The body measurement was 8' 4".

Bud, especially, hoped for a trophy-size bear. He got it in the monster shown with him above. Its skull, officially measured at 29 7/16 inches, placed well up on the record list.

A thumb rule used by the old Aleut bear hunters is that a bear with a body measurement of 8' 4" to 8' 6" will square out about ten feet. I find the thumb rule fairly accurate.

This may be the time to point out that the squared size of a bear is useful only for purpose of conversation. The accepted method of judging a trophy bear is by skull measurement, length and width added together. The lower jaw is removed and not considered in determining the skull size. A true reading is obtained through the use of mechanical devices in the hands of qualified persons designated by officials of the Boone and Crockett Club.

It is a simple matter to exaggerate a skin measurement in several ways. A bear can be skinned out in such a way that a "belly-flap" will increase its overall length by inches. Also, slight shifts in the hide as it is lying flesh side down can easily result in an untrue measurement.

Knowing all this, we of the bear hunting fraternity still speak of an eight-footer, a nine-footer or a ten-footer. It is a much easier way, when offering a client an estimate of the size of a bear under consideration, than to say to him, "Oh, it should run between 28 and 29 inches." That would sound incongruous in reference to a giant bear, as if we were talking about a small cub, and moreover, it is impossible for a guide to give a near-accurate estimate of the skull size.

Ken and Jim joined us shortly. After a period of examination and admiration, brief because of the late hour, the slow and somewhat difficult work of skinning the big animal began. It took all four of us to roll the animal around as the skinning progressed. Fortunately the bear had died on level, open ground. Any reputable guide takes pride in a proper skinning job for trophy preparation. The body and leg cuts must be made carefully. The head, of course, requires the critical field work.

Eventually the job was done. With the hide lashed securely on a packboard, I started up the steep canyon. The green skin of a trophy-size Kodiak bear may exceed 150 pounds, and this pack was one of the heavier ones. It was a tiring ascent. Dead grass impeded every step. Shoulder-high brush did not simplify matters. Midway to the top Kenneth relieved me of the pack and took it to the ridge where we decided to cache it for the night.

Weary but light-hearted, we hiked back to the dory for our return to camp and another of old Mel's delicious camp dinners. The dory, prized by many Alaskans, is an efficient means of transport. Though not fast, it offers safe travel in fairly rough water and requires a minimum of upkeep. When powered by a good outboard motor, a dory will carry hunters many miles and save countless footsteps.

Once back at the cabin and settled for the night, it was easy to turn in early and enjoy the well-earned luxury of sound sleep, although there were exciting moments to relive over coffee cups.

Next morning Larry Keeler, the packer, Jim, Bud and I returned for the big pack. Some of our enthusiasm had worn off, as no one relishes the thought of such hard work. A big bear hide such as Bud's can make the man in front of the packboard feel that his boots aren't strong enough to hold his feet inside them. Surely they will squash out through the sides of the boots! To the best of my knowledge that has never happened, but I guarantee you'll expect it should you ever attempt to pack a big hide.

As hunters, Bud and Jim were not expected to accompany us. They elected to do so, however, rather than spend a lazy day in camp. Fortunate it was for Jim. On the way in we spotted a beautiful bear. Jim and I took off after it while Larry, accompanied by Bud, went on after the pack.

It was a pleasure to see Jim perform in the same efficient manner with his .375 Magnum as his brother had performed the day before. After we completed a stiff climb to get within easy shooting range, he dispatched the bear quickly and humanely.

While Jim and I were experiencing all the thrills of a successful bear hunt, Larry was again demonstrating his capability and responsibility. A far cry from the fun we were having, Larry had shouldered the pack and carried it to the beach. As if that were not enough, he returned to help with Jim's bear. Larry is a strapping six-footer, and though not then a licensed guide, he was well qualified in all aspects of big game hunting. It has been a pleasure to me to watch him grow and mature from a gangling 'teen-ager into a responsible, respected man and fine registered guide.

By May third we had Bud's big bear hide fleshed and salted. Skin and rough skull measurements were recorded. The hide measured 9'8" from tip of nose to tip of tail. Across the front legs from claw to claw it was 10'5". The squared size, obtained by adding the two measurements and dividing by two, gave us a 10' 1/2" bear. There was not a blemish on it. The hair was dark brown, long and luxurious—a real beauty. Many hours were spent preparing the skull for official measurements, which would be made after the 60-day drying-out period specified by regulations. At the end of this period, Jonas Brothers of Seattle found the skull to be 29 7/16 inches—well up in the record list for the fourth edition of *Records of North American Big Game*.

The remaining days of the hunt went quickly. Bright sunshine and clear days were the order of the weather after the rainy beginning. When Jim's bear was fleshed and ready for shipment to the taxidermist, we were free to loaf, hunt hair seals, fish for sole, take pictures of the gorgeous scenery, eat and visit. We had counted 35 bears during our hunt, and all members of the party were at peace with the world.

A surprising amount of work is required to close a hunting camp at the conclusion of a hunt. The boats must be brought up to the cabin and stored bottom side up. All gear and materials must be appraised, inventoried and catalogued.

During this pleasant period, while we were waiting for the Grumman Widgeon to pick us up and return us to Kodiak, our happy-go-lucky mood was destroyed without warning. Old Mel, my faithful friend and employee, suffered a heart attack. A long, trying night followed, with all of us doing what we could. I thought how old Mel, just 10 short years before, had been a most ardent sheep hunter at the age of 64. Even now, Mel possessed a valid guide's license and

Jim's turn came the next day. A beautiful bear, he dispatched it quickly and humanely. He, Bud, Ken and Larry posed beside it before we started the skinning.

Bud and Jim, above, were thoroughly familiar with their rifles. That a gun should fit the hunter like an old shoe is a more important consideration than the caliber or the load.

was probably Alaska's oldest registered guide. He loved the hunting camp—the pleasures, the troubles, the successes, and the disappointments. It was a part of him. When the plane arrived the next day, Mel walked unassisted from the cabin and climbed aboard. We couldn't know that this was to be Mel's last hunt. He died a short time later.

A few comments about rifles, bullets and sighting equipment may be of interest to some. Bud was using a Model 70 .300 H&H magnum, firing his hand loads and a 250-grain Barnes bullet. This is a deadly outfit. Guides are frequently asked to recommend a caliber for certain specified game animals. From experience and from watching the results of my clients' shooting, the caliber is less important than proper bullet construction. Possibly the most important consideration is the hunter's familiarity with the weapon he is using. Few hunters can call their shots in the stress, strain and excitement of the hunt, but anyone using a gun that fits like an old shoe can be counted on to do a first class job. He may not place the bullets with minute angle accuracy, but he will certainly get them where they count.

Sighting equipment rates high on the list of things guides are asked about. Bearing in mind that all the areas inhabited by our Alaska brownies are subject to considerable rainfall, a receiver sight appears to be the answer unless a telescope sight is required as an aid to weak or failing eyesight. This is another of the rules which cannot be hard and fast. The telescope sight may fall into the class of the rifle that fits like an old shoe. Nevertheless, it is difficult to place an accurate shot hurriedly with a blob of water on either lens.

It was with genuine regret that I shook hands and said goodbye to Bud and Jim Piper in Kodiak. Our hunt had included everything any red-blooded sportsman could hope for. The parting regrets were softened when Bud assured me, "We'll give the Endicott Mountains a whirl next time, Hal."

I'm looking forward to that hunt. In a remote and wildly beautiful mountain range, in a grove of spruce trees, our sheep hunting camp will be 200 miles north of the Arctic Circle. Lake trout, pike and grayling will be lurking in the water, ready to oblige. I dream of the tundra grizzly, most prized of all our grizzlies, that we'll see fattening himself in the berry fields.

Yes, Bud, we'll give the Endicotts a whirl. ■

Brownie sow and her cub look at intruders.

61

Trout For A Texan

Dee gills an arm-length Dolly Varden on his first cast into the pool.

Story and photos by CHARLES J. KEIM

Reprinted from Alaska Sportsman® ,September, 1960 (ALASKA® magazine)

"Guess Ah've snagged a log, Chuck."

I looked at Hi Fi's line, which had settled in the middle of the stream above the pool Dee and I had been fishing.

"First log I've ever seen float upstream," I shouted, then quit shouting because the Texan simply wasn't listening. He was too busy fighting his fish, which by now had started moving toward the log jam. It was a big fish, I could tell because it broke water for a moment before it dived like a submarine.

Hi Fi gave it a little line, his casting rod bent like a buggy whip, and the fish was off to the races. Hi Fi stood his ground, clamped his teeth more firmly around his cigar, and gave and took line for about ten minutes. By that time Dee had put down his spinning gear and was watching too. We debated whether we should offer to net the fish. Hi Fi hadn't brought a net.

Finally the fish went into a series of frenzied leaps. Hi Fi ended our debate by placing considerable trust in his four-pound leader and horsing the fish ashore. It was a 23-inch king salmon, in good shape that promised equally good eating.

Hi Fi hoisted it by the gills and said in Texas talk what seemed to me a highly inadequate remark. "Yes, suh, that's quite an item."

I later learned, when Hi Fi caught more of these "items," that the imperturbable Texan had displayed unusual excitement.

I'd met Hi Fi and heard about his ambition to catch some of these items only the evening before this trip began. He happened along while I was loading my pack and fishing gear into the station wagon so everything would be ready next morning when Betty, my wife, would drive me to the depot. My party was scheduled to catch the Alaska Railroad train for Talkeetna, in south-central Alaska, then go aboard Cliff Hudson's riverboat up the Talkeetna River to the mouth of crystal-clear Clear Creek.

"You-all going fishing?" Hi Fi inquired, then added, after I'd answered that I was, "Mah wife, Travis, is here attending the Science Institute at the university. Ah plan to do some fishing, if Ah can find wheah to go." Then he introduced himself as H. F. Railsback, principal of Magoffin School in El Paso, Texas.

Fishermen understand fishermen. I was immediately sympathetic with Hi Fi's desires. I made some polite talk for a time, all the while wondering whether there was some way we could include him in our party.

I'd telephoned Cliff at the B and K Trading Store in Talkeetna and, after he'd assured me the fishing was "terrific," told him to expect eight men. Then I'd bought grub for eight.

We had special reasons for making up the party as we had. Major Louis Clark, assistant professor of military science and tactics with the Reserve Officers Training Corps, and SFC James Dixon, administrative assistant, were both ending their tours of duty in Alaska. Lou was going to Maine, Jim to Idaho, to new assignments, and both wanted a last, good fishing trip in Alaska to remember. Dr. Amo De Bernardis—Dee—was visiting professor of education. He wanted to do some fishing with long-time friend, Dr. Robert R. Wiegman, vice-president of the University of Alaska. Dee is superintendent of the Portland public schools. John Wiegman, thirteen, naturally wanted to go fishing with his father. Fred Boule, the university's director of athletics, had still to get in some real Alaskan fishing. Dr. Kenneth Young, dean of the faculty, had planned to come, but there was some doubt whether he could get away. I hadn't actually fished the

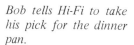

Bob tells Hi-Fi to take his pick for the dinner pan.

65

confluence of Clear Creek and the Talkeetna, but I'd done an "as told to" article about it and was eager to give it a try.

I hastily called Ken and learned that he would be unable to go. A few more calls gained an affirmative for my new friend, so I sent Hi Fi into Fairbanks fast to get a fishing license before the stores would close.

This was a riverboat operation with plenty of room for rods and gear.

It was Dee who named the Texan Hi Fi. Next morning after we'd clambered aboard the train, I introduced him and commented that his initials were easy to remember because I associated them with high frequency.

"Hi Fi is shorter, anyway," Dee said, so Hi Fi it was.

Cliff was waiting for us at the Talkeetna station after our eight-hour trip, which went surprisingly fast because the scenery is breathtaking and chiefly, because Bob improved our knowledge of the intricacies of gin rummy. Cliff piled some of the gear and half the party into his riverboat, and about an hour and a half later returned for the rest. The earlier group had spotted a grizzly along the riverbank, he said, but the bear was in a hurry.

The tent was up when we arrived, and camp was fairly well established on a high bank at the confluence of the two streams. We each placed a two-bit piece in a pool for the man who would catch the largest fish, then started limbering up our casting arms.

Bob and Dee went upstream. So did Fred and Lou. I stuck with John and Hi Fi. Jim played it lone wolf for a while. My first cast brought in an eighteen-inch grayling, which I promptly turned loose. In half an hour I'd caught and turned loose my limit in rainbows, Dolly Vardens and grayling. No use for me to save any "eating fish." We'd have plenty for a late-hour feed—very late, because the sun stayed up until far into the night.

I had two pots of coffee steaming on the gasoline stove when the others began straggling into camp. Fred and Lou had the largest string of trout, so heavy they'd actually rafted it downriver on a stringer.

"No more keepers tonight," Jim declared. "We've even got fish for breakfast."

There's no arguing with a sergeant, even if he's your friend. Besides, Jim was right. We had plenty of eating fish, too large for our cast-iron frying pan. Bob prepared them a la Wiegman. He placed a strip of bacon, a slice of onion, salt and pepper inside each fish, then wrapped them individually in two thicknesses of aluminum foil and placed them on the coals. He turned them after seven minutes, and served them eight minutes later.

We'd anticipated the usual exchange of fishing experiences around the campfire about midnight, but deferred the ritual when we had a visitor. He was Dan Pobar, come to meet the men who were fishing in his "front yard" and invite them to use the tent he had erected for such visitors.

"Thirteen other fellows and I came here in 1926, looking for gold," Pobar told us, answering our question. "We walked from Seward to Kantishna to Clear Creek. When we didn't find gold we split up. Three of us stuck together and decided we'd become trappers, but we didn't know much about trapping. We pooled our money, bought six traps, and caught thirteen mink—not a very good winter showing, even for amateurs. A couple of years later we bought traps, lots of them, for the beaver, mink and marten. They were plentiful and we did okay."

He still traps by himself, he explained, puffing reflectively upon a hand-rolled cigarette, although fur prices are away down compared to the old days. Then, beaver brought an average price of $70, mink $45, and marten $115, compared with today's $22, $12 and $7, respectively. He offered Bob a puff, which was accepted, then said something ought to be done about fur prices.

By that time we were all interested in his cigarette holder, which he explained was made from the front leg-bone of a "link."

"I get along here okay," he told us. "I trap and fish a little, and my meat supply walks right into the front yard. I'm building a cabin now to replace the one that burned down a couple of years ago. No rush, no pressure. I'm sixty-nine now and I plan to be hanging around here until I'm at least a hundred."

He explained the coal we'd seen in the river bed and along the banks. "It comes from a large seam about two miles upriver," he said. "I'll be collecting a couple of tons for my winter fuel."

Pobar said he could speak seven languages but didn't have much opportunity to use English, let alone the other six. Bob and Dee tried him on German and Italian and they conversed with apparent ease, until we decided we'd better hit the sack if we planned to go fishing early the next morning. It was early morning already.

Several of us pulled sizable trout from the river in front of camp after breakfast, then individually and in pairs began fishing upstream. That's when Hi Fi caught his first really big "item," and Dee and I pulled two-and three-pound rainbows from the pool below him.

Spring floods had piled up a formidable jam of logs, and much of their lengths had remained in a jumbled mass in the pool when the waters receded. I ventured onto one of the larger cottonwood logs and peered into the depths. Several large shapes moved slowly in and out of the shadows. The shadows were fish, but an angler would have to risk losing some tackle if he tried for them.

Fred, John, Lou, Bob, Dee, Hi-Fi, and Jim dine high on the hog with trout fillets.

"We'll have to keep their heads up once they're hooked," Dee commented. I nodded. Given half a chance, those fish would weave our six-pound monofilament in and out of the logs and free themselves.

Dee removed his 2 3/4-inch Dardevle from his line and put on his largest spoon, a 3 1/2-inch Dardevle. Its weight carried it quickly toward the bottom of the clear but turbulent pool. A rainbow carried it more quickly right back to the surface, and kept going about three feet into the air.

"You've got his head up," I shouted to Dee, "but don't try to keep it that high!"

The trout started plowing then, straining for the log jam where he could do some weaving. Dee stepped into a precarious position on the

Hi Fi looks over his first big fish.

log. His rod bent as he tugged cautiously to keep the trout fighting near the surface. The trout responded for a time and then, when Dee had to give some line, headed again for the log-strewn depths.

"You'll have to net this baby, and fast, Chuck," Dee said.

I picked my way through the logs until I was finally standing in a fairly quiet backwater below Dee's log. I told Dee, who couldn't see all of me, to ease off on the fish a bit, and I tried to take it by the tail—willing to forego proper netting procedure for expediency. The maneuver didn't work. Dee had to slug out a second round in a bout that had but one rule—keep fighting.

"It's your turn, Chuck," Dee said after I scooped the trout—head first.

We got three repeats from that pool, looked over Hi Fi's growing and proudly displayed catch, then headed half a mile upstream. We caught a couple of nice rainbows in some riffles before we came to another pool with its share of log hurdles.

We took turns, Dee first, connecting with and keeping a hard-fighting Dolly as long as his arm. Then the rainbows hit—one, two, three and up to eight—all putting on aerial performances we'll be dreaming about until we get to Clear Creek next time.

We dug into my tackle box, blew the dust off some small bucktails I'd tied eight years earlier for use in the Elwha River of the Olympic Peninsula and the Madison in Montana, crimped a couple of BB shot a foot above the flies and sank them below the white water entering the pool. The current carried the flies into the far reaches of the pool, and that's where the trout were hiding.

We left some gaps in our limits and headed leisurely back toward camp, some coffee, a big fish fry and some talk around the campfire.

"I even caught them with orange peel!" Fred exclaimed. "In twenty minutes I caught, weighed and freed three fish that weighed more than four pounds apiece! In four years of fishing in Colorado, I never had it like today!"

"First place I've ever fished where you'd throw back foot-long trout," Dee added.

"Ah've neveh seen anything like it!" Hi Fi declared, showing us his fish. "Man, what Ah'd give to show these to the folks back home!" ■

A Kodiak For A Texan

Ray tells Hal he's mighty pleased with his trophy.

By HAL WAUGH

What do you do when you're a 66-year old Texan and you've been wanting to get one of the world's largest bears from the largest state, 3500 miles away, since the day you were first able to straddle a bronc?

Ray Jennings of Hondo, Texas asked himself that question and answered it in the direct Texan way—he got the Kodiak bear, but it took some real doing, because even a Texan can't surmount all those challenges as casually as he decides to do so.

I'd guided Ray for two days in the Deadman Bay area of Kodiak Island, home of the world's largest bear, before we had established the hunters' kinship that breaks down the usual reserves. But when he said, "Hal, I'd give up any of my trophies, even my elephant, for a big ol' Kodiak," I wondered if he really meant it.

"Ray, that surprises me a little," I told him. "I've always admired the Kodiak, but didn't expect such enthusiasm from a man with your wide experience. I'm especially interested to learn that you rate it above everything else you've hunted."

"Every time I thought I had things put together, and could make the trip to Alaska, something happened." Ray continued, "I finally decided that this year just had to be it. Guess it's purty hard to understand just how bad I've wanted a Kodiak bear."

From the first time he had straddled that bronc, 60 years earlier, Ray had hunted in Africa, British Columbia, Mexico, Colorado, Wyoming, and his home state of Texas. So, he had hunting experience plus to draw from.

For the first day of Ray's hunt I had taken him to one of the canyons leading off Deadman Bay. The choice of location wasn't good. This particular terrain might be suited to a long legged fellow, but the short Texan legs weren't trained to step high enough for the toes to clear the spongy muskeg. Ray tripped innumerable times, but regained his footing each time with a smile.

"Doggone, I've hunted thorn bush in Africa, shintangle in Mexico, 10,000 foot altitude in Colorado, but I've never run into anything like this muskeg." He quickly added, "I'm not complainin'. I'd walk on my hands if I had to, to get me a big ol' Kodiak."

74

Earl Stevens, one of my guides, had accompanied us this day and I had a premonition that one of the three of us would spot a bear before long—just one of those feelings a guide experiences occasionally. Sure enough, when we were well up in the valley, nearing a lookout spot that I intended to use for the day, I spotted a bear slowly feeding and moving around the side of the mountain.

"Hey, there's a bear," I whispered to Ray.

"Where? Where is he? Lemme see. Point him out. Waited a long, long time for this!"

Gone was that slow Texan talk. Ray literally punctured the air with questions and exclamations. It was difficult to slow him down long enough to give him an answer.

"Look, take it easy and sight over my arm to see where I'm pointing."

Keen-eyed Earl quickly located the bear.

Then Ray spotted the bear. "Isn't he a dandy though, and purty, too. How big do you reckon he is, Hal?"

I honestly couldn't tell. Earl and I would have to work out a plan that would take us closer to the bear for a better look. Any mature Kodiak bear is big, but even at this distance it was evident that this bear was not one of the huge old timers. He was large enough to warrant this closer look because Ray hadn't asked for the largest animal on the island, just a good bear. The views we were able to get as bruin ambled through the occasional openings in the alders were too limited to enable us to determine his true size.

"Ray, I think we'll climb up the mountain for a while. Need to give you a rest from muskeg—and I agree we want a closer look at this one."

"Rest, climbin'?" He grinned. "Let's go feller."

Wind is the number one enemy of the bear hunter because the animal has a remarkable nose. Some areas are notorious for shifty winds and changeable air currents.

"Earl, why don't you go ahead of us and pick a way through the alders? We'll need to keep a screen of brush between us and that bear. But keep him in view."

"This is one of those tricky spots, but I'll see what I can do. Lost a bear here two years ago when the wind shifted," Earl replied.

We climbed cautiously, keeping clumps of alder and brush between us and the bear, ever alert for wind changes. Earl motioned for someone to light a cigarette, our old wind indicator.

Cigarette smoke, if used judiciously, makes the perfect wind indicator because the man making the stalk can keep constant watch of the wind and change course when necessary.

"There he goes! Darn it," lamented Earl.

The bear suddenly reversed his field and faded away into alder thickets, going in the opposite direction fast. We knew that some capricious breeze had carried a hint of danger to an extremely intelligent animal. At least he had given me time for a better look and I knew he was too small for a good trophy.

"Don't feel bad, Ray. He wasn't very large and we have plenty of time to get you a good trophy," I said.

"Feel bad? Wouldn't have missed it for the world. Wasn't he purty, and could he scat!" came from the friendly Texan.

Fun to hunt with a guy like that. High pressure builds up in a hunting camp very quickly at times, due to disappointments, desires for action, and multiple other reasons. It was evident as we made our way slowly back to the dory on the beach and down the bay to camp, that my hunter was both gentleman enough and sufficiently experienced to avoid the common difficulties. We'd get along.

The following day I chose a route that wouldn't necessitate climbing unless we had to go after a bear. The average hunter makes out better when the rough trips are thrown at him every other day. We spent the day strolling, with many restful stops to glass the mountainsides. Kodiak Island, where the weather can run to either extreme, was proving friendly.

"Texas can't beat this weather," Ray remarked as we viewed the sharp and clear skylines and watched the bright blue skies, dotted here and there with puffy cumulus clouds lazily drifting southward.

We enjoyed the weather on that second day of hunting, but we had no shooting. We watched several bear, none worth considering. After saying "too small" several times in answer to Ray's questions, I had to explain.

"Large bear or the real trophy sized fellows, seldom move quickly and never with jerky movements. It isn't that they are not capable of

Ray Jennings, left, and Larry Keeler look over the former's Kodiak bear hide.

great speed, but increased age seems to smooth out their actions. Too, another important factor to look for is the characteristic swinging movement of large bear. It appears that they swing head, body, and legs in a rhythmic manner. Nice to watch," was my explanation to Ray.

"So that's the way you tell? Coupla' those bear looked as big as a house to me. Hmmm."

We returned to camp, two satisfied and rested hunters.

May 24th arrived like any other sunshiny morning. We could not know that by evening we would have experienced slow difficult climbing, exhilaration, and a repetition of the previous day's lazy pleasure.

I had decided we'd hunt a canyon we call "Larry's Canyon" in appreciation of Larry Keeler, my efficient and loyal packer-guide crew member. Somewhat like the location of yesterday's hunt, Larry's

Canyon could be either tough or easy, depending entirely on where we'd spot a bear and if we decided to try for him.

Reaching our lookout was the signal for concentrated effort with binoculars. I strained my eyes, paying special attention to the lower reaches of the surrounding mountains. By late May the larger bear start to work the lower alder patches. Earlier in the year few large bear stay low, rather they favor the mountaintops or the maze of huge boulders and cliffs just below the top.

Soon after lunch I spotted a very large bear feeding in an alder thicket about 600 yards away and uphill from the lookout.

"Ray, there's our bear. I'm going to aim my rifle at him and I want you to locate him over my barrel."

"OK, lemme look. I can see 'im," came his quick reply.

Ray was much calmer than on the first day. More matter of fact. I considered it a good sign. He still wanted the bear just as much—it wasn't that, but two dry days had helped.

The bear apparently had been bedded down in the alders and had just arisen because I had carefully scrutinized this particular area earlier. It was good bear cover; the alders which by now were almost fully leafed out could screen the movements of game.

I waited. Came the expected and usual question, which I sidestepped.

"How big is he, Hal?"

Too often the hunter becomes unduly excited and eager if he learns the quarry is exceptionally large. This bear was.

"Ray it is going to be a tiresome sneak. He's a good bear, but we'll have to make the stalk slowly and carefully." I couldn't take a chance on exciting Ray; couldn't let him know my inner excitement for I felt the Texan deserved this trophy that he rated even above the elephant.

The wind had been blowing steadily up canyon from the bay all day. Providing my 66-year old hunter could make the climb, the odds looked good for a successful climax. The big bruiser bear was unintentionally cooperating by feeding into the wind, but slowly gaining altitude. If the bear fed slowly and we climbed swiftly, Ray should get shooting.

Climbing is never easy. A mountainside that looks smooth from the bottom often has a succession of drainage gullies and ravines which tax even the youngest of legs.

We climbed steadily, working into the wind towards the bear. It seemed that we would never gain an open hillside for easier walking.

"Are you all right Ray" I'd ask occasionally. He would answer affirmatively with a game smile. I had instructed Ray to stop any time he felt the need, and I had impressed on him that I would wait for him. He should do nothing that would overtax his heart or cause any bodily damage.

Ray was proving something I'd long contended—any age can hunt, if he uses good sense. And that's one of the principal reasons I was enjoying this hunt.

An hour and a half later we reached a spot directly uphill from where I had last seen Mr. Bear. He was either bedded down again or he had moved into another alder patch. There was nothing to do but sit down and wait him out.

"Ray, don't be too disappointed if we never see this bear again. There are so many ways he can walk away without our seeing him."

"Oh, I don't think so Hal. . . . We have been mighty careful and you have been lookin' all the time. We'll get him alright."

The confidence displayed by my client was reassuring in a way as it indicated that when the big show would come, he would be calm and efficient. However, I knew from past experience a sudden change in wind direction carrying the hunter's scent towards the bear, would spook him out, or his natural feeding habits might lead him through some ravine, brush choked and hidden to the observer's sight.

We were situated in a grassy, open location with a panoramic view of the entire mountainside and valley below us. I noted several jutting frost heaves we could utilize to hide our movements if we located the bear and had to make a sneak on him. Leaving Ray in a comfortable position, I gradually worked with great care towards the spot where we had last observed the bear. A few feet, then use the glasses. This was slow cautious work. Any quick movement could have been disastrous. That bear was too big and the climb had been too difficult for an older man to risk wasting an opportunity through lack of caution.

Moments like this age a guide. Had I made a mistake? If so, when and where? How could we have performed the sneak in any other manner?

One particular brush ravine extending from the flat of the valley to the top of the brush line had fascinated me from the beginning of our climb. I had felt that such a ravine held many possibilities for the bear and had called this to Ray's attention. A rocky cliff resembling a sawtooth bordered the ravine on the bay side. Time and again I had studied the area through the binoculars. Turning my head for another look now, I was rewarded with a memorable sight of the big bear. "Wow," I mumbled to myself. "We have to get this one." He looked monstrous and prime. Best of all he was unaware of our presence. Our stealthy approach had paid off.

The big fellow had fed through the alders from where we had last seen him, worked uphill in the ravine and was now climbing out and would soon cross over the sawtooth ridge and be lost to us.

Heart hammering with excitement, I looked uphill at Ray. Fortunately, Ray turned to look down in my direction just as I began making frantic motions in an attempt to show him the bear. Of all times for a hunter to miss seeing game! Ray could not see this bear.

I climbed back up the hill so hurriedly that when I reached Ray I was too winded to speak. All I could do was grunt and point.

My little Texan client suddenly spotted the Kodiak, and told me afterwards that he simply couldn't understand why he hadn't seen him quicker.

"Guess I was just tryin' too hard. Didn't know too well what I was lookin' for and I know I was lookin' too low. Sorry Hal."

There was no time for Ray to even comment on the bear's size. The Texan had an estimated 45 seconds to swivel around and rest his rifle over a convenient hummock for a prone shot that was as comfortable and steady as shooting could be.

The scope-sighted .300 H&H roared.

"He's hit. Shoot again."

The second shot connected also, but through my binoculars I couldn't be positive where the wounds were. The third shot was a clean miss. The bear seemed to hang on the side of the mountain then,

80

slowly at first, began to slide and lose his grip, finally ending in a tumble that took him out of sight to the brink of the ravine.

Every experienced rifleman has felt both complete confidence and satisfaction following the shooting episode. Also he has experienced the slight nagging feeling of incompleteness or dissatisfaction following the shooting. I had this nagging worry now. For some reason I felt upset and told Ray.

"Darn it, I have to go up there and dig that bear out of the alders. A helluva' job."

"I'll go right along with you, boy," said the 66-year old to the 50-year old. Usually I prefer to do this distasteful and dangerous task alone, unless my guides, Earl, Larry or Joe are with me. Now I just told Ray that we would climb higher and get in a better position.

About 50 yards higher and five minutes later, the awesome sight of a huge, wounded and very angry bear appeared. He was weaving some, but full of life and spunk. I still couldn't tell where he had been hit, but he was vindictive. The course of travel he had chosen was complete proof. He had climbed out of the steep ravine to get to his enemies, rather than run downhill to probably escape.

We were slightly lower than the bear, but modern high power rifles offset any advantage that his bulk, courage, and position could muster. If Ray had any difficulties in stopping him, there was always "Big Nan," my .375 Weatherby which has earned quite a reputation as a "stopper" over many seasons.

"For gosh sakes, take him," I pleaded.

"Where shall I hit him?" Ray queried, wanting to do everything right.

"Anyplace in the front quarters, but for Pete's sake start shooting!"

Ray poured out three shots, each one taking effect as the big bear bellowed in anger and frustration. With a last mighty heave he expired and slid downhill into another alder ravine.

The shooting was over and Ray had one of the world's finest trophies. Despite age, steep mountains, brush, and a 40-year waiting period, he had his Kodiak bear.

Our approach to the downed bear was very careful. We remembered the pure viciousness and unbelievable vitality the bear

81

had displayed. Once above him in the alders, I tossed a few small rocks down on him, but he was dead.

"No hurry now, Ray," I cautioned my anxious client, "I'll just give him a poke or two with a stick before we get too near." I did this, holding the stick in my left hand and "Big Nan" pistol-like in my right.

After making positive he was dead, we both relaxed enough to shake hands and pound each other on the back. The animal was plainly too heavy for two men to handle and skin out so I made what body cuts I could, leaving the skinning for the next day when I would return with Larry. Though we couldn't roll bruin over, we found no rubbed spots, the bane of spring bear hunters.

The next day we picked an easier route to our bear and a few hours later we were back in camp busy at fleshing.

I was somewhat disappointed with the skull measurements for we found that it scored only 28". This will place the bear in the record book. But the true size of this bear can be seen in Hondo, Texas, in the form of a huge rug.

We found the fleshed hide laying flat, flesh side down, measured 11' 3½" from tip of claw to tip of claw across the shoulders. The tip of nose to tip of tail measurement was 9' 2½" for a squared size of 10' 3".

"Ray, do you still want a Kodiak more than any trophy in the world?" I asked as we drank coffee and looked proudly at the big and perfect pelt laying out on the grass. And I added, "How do you like the largest state in the Union?"

"Hal, I wouldn't trade this bear for my elephant, no, nor for my lion, buff, and rhino thrown in," he answered, "and your state, it's wonderful." Although that was quite an admission for a Texan, I believed him. ∎

Hidden Valley Grayling

The canoe can go where fish almost need dust goggles, but a heavy load and a shallow stretch have author on the pulling end of the painter.

Story and photos by CHARLES J. KEIM

Reprinted from Alaska Sportsman®, March, 1960 (ALASKA® magazine)

Fred Machetanz, artist, writer, lecturer and photographer, adjusted his tripod, took a final meter reading and shouted, "Okay!"

Frederick Boyle, athletic director at the University of Alaska where I'm journalism and English prof, cast his Royal Coachman into the stream at the same time as I put in a mosquito. Then we forgot that Fred was taking movies.

Frederick gave his line a quick jerk to set the hook. His gear started downstream as his new, lightweight glass rod bent into an exciting arc. I quit watching when my tackle began doing the same. I gave line for a while, then started taking it in as my grayling headed toward me, surfaced again, kicked up a spray with its whole body and gave up. I brought it to my landing net.

"Don't step in Frederick's way," Fred shouted, "he's still busy."

I removed the hook from my grayling, which measured about

85

twelve inches. When Fred shouted, "Okay," I looked at my fishing partner. He was examining the huge dorsal fin of a fifteen-incher.

"Well, Fred," I said with a grin, "do you think you're going to get your grayling movie?"

"No question about that," he replied, then added the characteristic remark of a good photographer, "I hope the sun will hold out."

There was reason to worry about the sun. The spring and summer were unusually cloudy and rainy. No reason to worry about getting fish in my hidden valley. It always had produced grayling much larger than those Frederick and I had just caught. That is why I'd recommended the place to Fred.

"I'm looking for a place where I can get a good color movie of grayling fishing to show on our lecture tour," he had explained when he visited the campus the previous fall. "That will wind up my movie-making. From then on we plan to paint and write at High Ridge, our place near Palmer."

Fred is the sort of person I like to cooperate with. For years he and his wife, Sara, have traveled about Alaska, territory and state, photographing, painting and writing, then going on a regular winter movie-lecture circuit down south to tell hundreds of thousands of people about the Great Land they both love.

"I know the place," I said. "I call it my hidden valley. Oh, a few others get in there occasionally, but you really have to work to do it. Best grayling fishing I've found in Alaska."

"Where is it?"

"Somewhere in the Alaska Range. A friend showed it to me, and a friend had shown it to him. We don't mean to be selfish about it, but we did promise to be discreet. Any sportsman will understand why. Can you make a movie without pinpointing the location?"

"You bet!"

After the summer session we were ready to go. I asked Frederick Boyle to come along, as he likes to fish as well as I do and he's an excellent canoeist. He is generally called Fred too, but I thought two Freds on a trip could get confusing.

"I'll be Frederick," he agreed.

My 19-foot square stern Grumman aluminum canoe was heavily loaded when we put into the water, but the prop of the 7½

Boyle displays the reason for discretion about the valley's location. Grayling like this are worth the effort of getting to them.

horsepower outboard took hold and the craft balanced nicely when we hit the first haystacks. We'd battened down everything except Fred's camera. He was soon busy using it, and finding his life jacket a bit troublesome. But we were glad to be wearing them, and at times it was reassuring to know that the canoe had flotation chambers bow and stern.

From time to time we had to jump out and tow the canoe when the stream shallowed. We didn't mind. I prefer the canoe to the more common riverboat because you can take the canoe where a fish almost needs dust goggles, though admittedly the riverboat is larger, more stable and better suited to cope with the toughest waters.

Fred got footage of the towing operations while we joked that he "had figured things out nicely." Actually, we rotated so each man had his turn at just walking along.

Both Fred and Frederick soon learned why I had fastened the end of an apple box to the canoe's stern with two large C clamps. With the motor mounted on this improvised transom, the propeller was almost even with the keel rather than down where it could strike logs, rocks or bottom. Then, too, we had deliberately loaded the canoe a bit bow-heavy, so the bow would usually ground in shallow water before the propeller would strike.

"There's a caribou," Frederick said during one of our refueling stops.

The animal, his rack in the velvet, shambled almost to the riverbank opposite us. The wind was in our favor. The caribou lifted his head and fixed his eyes on us, trying to determine what had invaded his land.

Far behind him, high mountain peaks blanketed with new snow competed for our attention. Below timber line on the nearer hills, green birch leaves had already started changing to gold which contrasted sharply with the dark spruce and harmonized with the mosaic of smaller growth and lichens.

We watched quietly, not so much fearing to spook the caribou as to profane a setting in which only the stream's song was fitting sound.

The caribou turned broadside and trotted away, shaking his head from side to side as though he, too, felt the wonderment of it all.

"Let's go," I said. "If you like this, you'll like my valley even better. It's just around that bluff."

We all were glad of that. We were tired, somewhat wet from splashing along in the stream, and eager for Fred to get as much footage as possible while the sun shone.

The stream began to narrow as we neared the valley. Confident that we wouldn't ground, I put on more power and the canoe pushed aside the small haystacks that were starting to form. As these heightened I added more power, yet held back a reserve for possible emergency. At times the canoe remained motionless in the tumult of water, and even retreated stern-first as the turbulence intensified. My main task was to keep the bow into the current.

A trick I'd learned from watching grayling, trout and salmon in fast water helped me. I'd noticed that the fish would continue to move their fins and tails furiously even when the current would stop them completely. Then, as the current would shift or lessen for a moment, the fish would shoot ahead repeating the process until they would reach quieter water.

We did this with the canoe, my companions paddling at times of greatest pressure. Then we entered the valley.

We were greeted by a flock of ducks on a small lake alongside the stream. Those which had completed the molt rose from the water and seemed to climb one of the valley's sloping walls. Then they circled us once, gained more altitude, and flew toward a lake at the distant end of the valley—our objective, too, before we would turn back toward civilization. The rest of the ducks, those still lacking their flight feathers, paddled toward the grassy bank, the small V's they printed on the surface punctuated by swirls of rising grayling.

We pushed into the lake. Frederick and I rigged our fishing gear while Fred set up his camera on the stream bank. Then he photographed our first successful casts.

We saved six of the largest grayling and a hook-damaged smaller one, then moved upriver to one of my camping spots. There we broiled our grayling while the heavy shadow of one valley wall inched up the slope of the other and the snow on the peaks turned rose in the setting sun.

"We'll keep base camp here," I said, "and with the canoe lighter we'll be able to move easily to the best fishing locations."

"Is this a good one?" Frederick asked when the camp chores were over.

"Yes."

"Well, I'm going to catch us some breakfast."

He did just that, then climbed one of the valley walls while Fred and I built a large fire, outlined our next day's plans, then stacked more wood on the fire to help guide our companion home.

Fred looked apprehensively at the low bank of clouds which peered over the distant peaks next morning.

"Are we going to get rain, Chuck?"

"Nope. We've waited a year for this trip and nothing's going to spoil it. Those clouds just want to see what's going on." I broke the ice which had formed in the coffee pot during the night, hoping I was right.

I was. By the time the coffee was boiling and we'd kicked Frederick out of the sack, a morning breeze had cleared the sky and we could enjoy our breakfast of grayling, bacon, coffee and fresh blueberry pancakes without weather worries.

As we ate we watched a cow moose doing the same in a fringe of willows across the stream.

"I'll bet there's good moose hunting here," Fred said.

"Grizzly bear, too," Frederick said. "I learned that last night. In a cleared area on the side of the valley I found a number of ground squirrel holes, then places where something had dug others out. Finally I ran into the grizzly tracks, fresh, bigger than my boot, and going uphill too. I finished my climb with my .44 Ruger magnum in my hand."

Machetanz (left) and Boyle lunch heartily on grayling broiled in aluminum foil.

90

"Ever spot the bear?" I asked, mindful of a few similar experiences in the valley.

"No, I'm happy to say."

We put our grub in one pile, gear in another, spread plastic sheets over both and headed upstream with a more buoyant canoe.

As we penetrated deeper and deeper into the valley, we noticed more beaver lodges, some towering high above the bank. We encountered several beavers dragging willows through the water. Often we could see the branches they'd anchored deep in the stream.

"They're starting to put in cold weather supplies already," Fred observed. "I imagine winter is a rough season here."

"Yes, but it brings the animals into the valley. Moose, especially, come here from the hills to feed on all this willow."

The stream began to spread and we were forced to tow the canoe. There were grayling everywhere, lying motionless and facing upstream in the deeper pools, and fanning out ahead of us as we trudged through the water, their huge dorsal fins at times actually breaking the surface.

"You could get them here with a rock!" I remarked.

"Let's just get some," Frederick replied. "How far is it to this lake, anyway?"

"At the base of that cliff."

Now the water was deeper and more turbulent and formed a huge V as it flowed from the lake. I steered the canoe into the vertex of the V and, as we started uphill, put on almost full power. We moved ahead for a time, then gradually the canoe slowed until it became motionless in the torrent. For a short while we sat there. Then I coaxed a bit more power from the motor. The canoe inched forward then slowed again to a standstill, for by now we were riding atop a peculiar crest formed by water flowing laterally on either side into the main funnel, which spilled from a build-up of rocks at the very edge of the lake.

For the first time I shoved on full power. The canoe moved ahead, poised uphill for a moment half in the lake and half in the current. My companions dipped the paddles, and suddenly we were skimming over the lake. I cut the power, but not before the noise of the motor, rocketing through the bowl and bouncing from the high cliff, startled a flock of ducks.

"That is a rather interesting final obstacle," Fred commented as we stepped ashore. "Where should we set up?"

"Right at the obstacle. The big ones feed at the outlet."

Frederick cast a tiny fly far out into the lake, then set the hook as a large grayling arced half out of the water and down onto the fly. The fish sounded, then began pulling for the far shore with Frederick grudgingly giving line. The fish slowed, then suddenly darted at an angle of almost ninety degrees for the outlet. Had he reached it, even a fisherman of Frederick's skill would have had a hard time stopping him. Frederick's rod bent far to the left then and he paid out and took up line carefully. The fish cleared the water three times, almost like a rainbow trout, then the fight went out of him and Frederick reeled him in.

Fred, meanwhile, had been setting up his camera.

"Now, if you can do that again so I can get the action on film, I'll count this wonderful, sunny expedition a success," Fred said.

"It'll be fun to try," Frederick answered, and the fish cooperated splendidly for all three of us until Fred announced that he had all the footage he would need.

"Then we'll batten down everything except your movie camera, Fred," I said. "You'll want to use it to show the change of pace on the downstream trip."

I used the motor to push us to the outlet, then tilted it up and took a paddle. Frederick sat in the bow and Fred amidships. Our ejection through the funnel set the pace for much of the trip back to base camp. The canoe was even lighter now, as we had used gas to go upstream. With the shallower draft we were able to ride stretches in which we'd towed the canoe earlier. When only one man was needed to steer, Frederick would pick up his rod, catch a grayling, then grab a paddle again when the stream would liven its pace.

There's a special joy in canoeing, even in the larger craft, when one has a skilled canoeist as a partner. Sitting in the bow, Frederick telegraphed his messages to me over the almost nineteen-foot distance by just the right motion of his body as he prepared to dig into the water, whether for propulsion or steering, and he proved especially

Boyle (checked shirt) helps photographer Machetanz unload equipment. Thousands will "take" the trip later by way of the resulting movies.

adept at back-paddling for careful steerage around some of the water-lashed boulders in the wilder stretches.

Virtually tireless, he climbed the other side of the canyon when we arrived at base camp that evening. Fred and I, with binoculars, watched his progress alternately with the ramblings of a moose and her calf coming down to the more plentiful willow growth along the stream.

Next morning we headed downstream again, pausing at times to enable Fred to get footage of ducks and beavers, closer now because there was no motor noise, and scenery still basking in strong sunshine. Frederick and I caught some grayling to take home.

Clouds were beginning to form when we returned to the campus, and they were dumping their rain on us as we said goodbye to Fred.

"I'll let you know how the film turns out," Fred promised.

Soon afterward Frederick and I received a letter saying, "It turned out beautifully!" And I guess it did, for we are receiving essentially the same message from people in the lower 49 who, through the magic of Fred's movie, have gone after grayling in my hidden valley. ∎

94

Jackpot Hunt

Beautiful Wild Lake, a hundred miles north of the Arctic Circle, is surrounded by summits of the Endicott Mountains.

Story and photos by HAL WAUGH

Reprinted from Alaska Sportsman® , October, 1958 (ALASKA® magazine)

We were sitting around the campfire 200 miles north of the Arctic Circle, on a hunt for Dall sheep trophies.

Several days of beautiful early fall weather had suddenly turned to softly falling snow, and if we were to take our trophies and keep our later date with the mountain goats of the Kenai several hundred miles to the south, we had come to the conclusion that we had better end our dallying as tourists and become hunters.

"Dad," observed Dr. John Seidensticker, of Twin Bridges, Montana, "I think we should take the best looking rams out of the next bunch we see."

95

In Dr. John, and his father, Jack, I had really drawn aces in the always unpredictable game of guide work. They were big and strong. They were gentlemen and real sportsmen. They were a joy to guide.

In the months of planning prior to the hunt, we had decided on an ambitious schedule that would produce sheep from the Endicotts, far north of the Arctic Circle, goats from the Kenai on Alaska's southerly coast, and whatever else showed up in the sights at opportune moments.

Our camp was now on the John River, deep in the Arctic range. Earl Stevens and I had flown in a few days before the arrival of the Seidenstickers, and had set up a comfortable tent camp in a grove of spruce timber. The weather was ideal—clear and warm during the days yet crisp enough at night to warrant good sleeping robes.

By the time Jack and John arrived we had scouted the area, located good grayling fishing spots, and cut wood for the campfires to come and for the little Yukon stove on which Earl produced miracles in the way of tasty camp dishes.

The Endicott Mountain country is a surprise to any hunter who has not seen it. Once on top of a mountain, the going is easy. It's like a cow pasture in places, not what one would expect for mountain sheep hunting. The rolling hills are covered with grass and flowers. Yet the area is home to one of the heaviest concentrations of Dall sheep in North America.

The task, once you are located on a river, is to reach the smooth, rolling terrain on top. The valleys of much of our northern hunting country have a covering of muskeg, that spongy, squashy, exasperating bog. It presents a slow and tiring route to the mountaintops, where it gives way to firmer footing. We were one and a half hours of almost tortuous travel from our riverside camp to reasonably good hiking ground.

James L. Anderson, pilot and station manager for Wien Alaska Airlines at Bettles Field, had flown our party in to camp. The little 170 Cessna, with an outside load limit of five hundred pounds when equipped with floats, had performed admirably even when taxed to its limit. The Seidenstickers weigh in at 225 and 250 pounds. What a load of men!

96

The first few days of hunting in the upper reaches were rewarding, but the breaking-in process was an ordeal for Dr. John. Not so for Jack, a tough old working cowboy who had never learned how to take it easy—even after a life-time of hard work had rewarded him with a successful ranch stocked with registered Herefords.

We saw sheep now and then, in varying numbers. The rams were in small groups or alone. One pleasant episode will remain long in my

Hal with "wings" of massive moose horns.

memory. Four rams, one a fairly good trophy with a full curl, were traveling and grazing together. The old gentleman under consideration reached a protected ledge which offered a good lookout, a suitable spot for his midday rest. With a series of characteristic maneuvers he pawed out a bed and carefully lowered himself into it, legs folded beneath his body. With miles and miles of beautiful mountain scenery to survey by merely turning his head slightly, he should have been good for an hour or so of rest.

His rest was not to be, however, as the youngest of the four rams decided this was the time for play. He opened the game with a few false charges at the old fellow, pulling up short each time just before contact. Feinting from the right, then from the left, he tried his attack. When all conditions were right, the youngster crashed head-on into the great ram's horns.

97

The blow apparently wasn't even a warm-up for a veteran of breeding season battles with mature opponents, as he seemed to take it casually. The big ram's patience soon wore thin, however, and in obvious disgust he arose from his bed and resumed feeding.

For Jack, Dr. John and me, the comic incident brought us a little closer to these beautiful animals and the routine of their everyday lives.

With days left to spend and sheep so plentiful, we decided that nothing short of outstanding trophy heads would satisfy us. Hunting of this kind is fascinating. It is a channel of adventure rarely attained. It is critical. The full beauty of the whole animal is considered. The young and vigorous are ignored and left to propagate the species. Sought after are the patriarchs who are approaching life's end.

To search out a fine trophy, stalk him successfully, dispatch him quickly and humanely, and take his distinctive beauty back home for the appreciation of many, is the trophy hunter's challenge.

The sturdy cabin at Wild Lake was good to come back to at the end of a crisp fall day.

On the mountaintops we selected comfortable lookouts and glassed the surrounding areas, all the time wondering what was on the slope just beyond.

Wolf sign was everywhere. Nature, however, appears to have a way of balancing the predator-game ratio. Our sheep count for this hunt was approximately 250, which would lead one to believe that the wolves had not decimated the Endicott Mountain sheep herds. A healthy lamb crop was everywhere in evidence.

The geography of the area is such that we could travel a circuitous route during the day and without a great deal of hiking return to our camp. Mountain ridges parallel the river, with creeks every few miles originating high on the mountains and rambling down to the river bottom. Through ages the creeks had cut deep canyons, which provide food and shelter for game animals. We tried to probe into each canyon as we came to it.

After several bright, sparkling days the skies turned dark and gray. Obviously the weather was changing. A fine mist gathered and turned into a gentle rain. In the high country, the rain became a downpour.

We were somewhat disturbed, but a snowstorm during an August sheep hunt seemed impossible even in the Arctic. The evening was cheerful enough. We responded heartily to Earl's production on the Yukon stove, and felt sorry for all the folks in the towns and cities. I believed we could take rams even in a storm, but could we manage to get the big trophies we all wanted?

The next morning we had it—snow! Obviously more was to come. The mountaintops were covered, affording poor background from our point of view—excellent background if you're on the side of the white sheep. Several inches of fresh snow didn't improve climbing conditions, and our clothing, limited by air travel to a remote location, was not the best for such weather.

We discussed every aspect of the situation and the hunters decided to go at it hard until two rams were down. When the desire for outstanding trophies was put aside, everything was fun again. We plowed across the muskeg and separated to hunt adjacent areas, agreeing to meet and hunt together in the afternoon.

Dr. John and Earl worked to the north while Jack and I made a long, easy swing to the east. As we were nearing the top, Jack had his first view of a wolverine. The largest member of the weasel family, the wolverine has somehow inspired more far-fetched tales than most of the world's other animals combined. This particular one, as I expected, wasted no time in putting distance between himself and us.

We saw the usual quota of ewes and lambs with a scattering of young rams, but nothing of pointed interest until some time after our meeting with Dr. John and Earl.

Then we saw three rams working away from us on a ridge to the north. The binoculars revealed that one was a good-sized ram with a full curl. Another, though not in the same class, was acceptable. The third was immature, with little more than a half curl.

This was just the type of situation we had looked for. With luck our chances of making an approach were good.

Through the soft snow we hiked, making good time. Fortunately for us the rams fed down the mountain toward the river, giving us a nearly direct route of approach. One of the small finger ridges extended down from the mountaintop and ended in a low rock cliff just above the sheep. If we could reach it undetected, the hunters would have easy, short shots.

I sent Earl a little to our left, thinking he might see the sheep before we could and direct us by hand signals to the most advantageous shooting position. Everything worked out as planned and Earl was soon motioning us on down the ridge. The sheep were obviously just below us. Crawling on hands and knees, we reached the top of the small cliff and saw the three rams feeding peacefully, unaware of any danger.

"Just tell me which one," said Jack.

It was easy to determine that the immature ram was out in front, so I whispered softly, "The last two."

"I'll take the last one, Dad," said Dr. John quickly, and fired. The ram went down for an instant kill. Just as quickly, Jack fired and killed the middle ram—the finer trophy, which Dr. John like the sportsman he is, had chosen for his father.

The value of constant practice and familiarity with one's rifle had been proved again. Jack had used his 30-S Remington, sporter, for many—more than twenty—years, and with it he is quick and deadly.

Later, in other areas, his moose, goat and black bear were each downed with a single shot.

The sudden death of his companions and the roar of rifle fire left the third ram confused and unable to decide which way to run. I frightened him off with the hope that he would be forever alert to the danger of man.

We skinned out the capes and dressed the sheep for the big pack. Going downhill is easier than climbing, but even with a pack board of the best design, a heavy pack means hard work. Yet there is no way to avoid back-packing in areas where pack animals are not available or cannot be used because of the terrain.

During the next few days, Earl and I were mainly occupied with fleshing out and salting capes and hanging the meat. Sheep meat is the choicest of all game. We fried and ate great quantities of delicious steaks and chops.

Wild Lake in the Endicott Mountains.

While we were busy, Jack and John were flycasting for grayling. A tasty fish of moderate size, the Arctic grayling is a welcome addition to the backwoods menu. It has a lingering suggestion of thyme, and a tendency to increase one's appetite. The grayling takes dry flies rapidly, usually at any hour of the day, the black gnat being its favorite.

As Andy, our pilot, was not due for a few days, we were free to take our pleasure as we found it. The John River valley in our vicinity is easy country to travel. We explored upstream and down, fishing occasionally and enjoying life.

101

We spotted two grizzlies, but in each instance the bear had every advantage. It was useless to try for them, so we contented ourselves with watching their wanderings through our spotting 'scopes.

Each was a perfect example of the northern grizzly, known by various names but in reality one and the same species. Their humps were prominent, their colors light above and dark brown on undersides and legs.

Andy was to fly over our camp when he made his weekly mail run to Anaktuvak Pass, so we could signal him if we wished. Knowing that Jack and John would enjoy a few days at Wild Lake, where there is a comfortable log cabin and the fishing leaves nothing to be desired, we watched for the mail run and flagged Andy down. The efficient bush pilot wastes little time. Before the day was over we were comfortably installed in the cabin at Wild Lake.

Beautiful Wild Lake, about eight miles long, is a hundred miles or so north of the Arctic Circle. On all but its south end it is bounded by picturesque mountains, its northern end opening into a rather narrow valley that eventually rises onto Tobin Mountain. A winter trail leads south from the lake along Wild River to Bettles Field.

This area was once the scene of a mild gold rush. Many of the old cabins are still there, though long past the habitable stage.

With the outboard motor Andy brought in for us and a borrowed boat that had been run up the sixty-odd miles of Wild River from Bettles some years before, we were able to fish and hunt with the assurance of a warm cabin and plenty of sheep steaks at night. Life was wonderful.

Jack had never killed a moose. We decided he should take one if we could find a good bull close enough to the lake to avoid long, heavy back-packing.

We saw several cow moose before we saw a suitable bull within our distance limit. Standing on the lake shore, he was just right and ever so much larger than the Shiras moose of Montana, Wyoming and Idaho, with which Jack was familiar.

So large an animal can absorb a lot of punishment. If only wounded, he may travel miles before dropping. This moose didn't even see us. He fell instantly to a well-placed, high lung shot which struck about ten inches below the back, directly behind the right shoulder.

When we dressed the bull we discovered that its right foreleg had once been broken, and had healed with only a slight enlargement of the bone to call attention to the break. Clients of mine have taken black bears, caribou and other moose that showed evidence of old fractures, and in each instance the animal was fat and in good condition. Nature is a skillful healer. Crippled animals do not necessarily fall to predators.

Sheep country in the Endicott Mountains.

While Earl and I took care of the meat and trophy, Jack and John enjoyed this fisherman's paradise. Wild Lake is teeming with lake trout, great northern pike and grayling.

The day finally arrived when we had to leave our happy hunting ground, as we hoped to hunt goats on the Kenai Peninsula hundreds of miles to the south.

I had set up the Kenai camp earlier in the summer, selecting the location because it was relatively undisturbed by hunters yet an excellent area for both goats and black bears. Dall sheep were plentiful for photographic purposes, too, as the area had then been closed to sheep hunting for six years.

The camp was a fairly short float-plane trip from Seward to a beautiful lake, then a forty-five minute hike up a valley. Directly in front of the cook tent was a natural spring which formed a pool eight feet in diameter. Fine gravel and sand bubbled constantly on the bottom as the water rose from the ground, clear, cold and tasteless.

During my absence of two months, one of the rather rare Kenai brown bears had used the tent frames as a rubbing post. We found plentiful evidence around camp that he considered the spot his temporary home.

Jack took a fine specimen of white mountain goat, a huge and bulky billy with heavy but not overly long horns. Dr. John also bagged his goat after some tiring climbs, which he claimed would condition him for either the ring or an old men's club. The Kenai Mountain country is so completely different from the John River country in the Endicotts that we felt we were on an entirely new hunt.

Jack was interested in getting a black bear, so after the goat capes were fleshed and salted for the trip to the taxidermist, we turned our attention to blackies. We saw several, but in each instance a great deal of time would have been consumed in making the necessary climbs. The blacks were feeding on the abundant growth of blueberries well above timber line, about three thousand feet in this area. The mountains are steep, rising from five hundred to almost five thousand feet without using much horizontal space.

At last we saw a shiny black patch bobbing along in the brush on a hillside. It could be only a black bear. The location was perfect for a stalk and the climb would not be bad.

It was nothing but fun, guiding Jack up on that bear. He had made so many stalks for deer and elk in his home state of Montana that he anticipated my every move. We worked carefully up and through the alders until, reaching a point above him, we sat down for a lesson in berry-picking from an expert.

104

An instinct seems to warn wild animals of danger at times when it is impossible for them to scent the hunter. Black bears are uncommonly well favored by this instinct. Time after time they will walk away from undetected danger when they are yet out of rifle range. This can be disconcerting to a hunter who has made a high climb and has the wind in his favor.

Without warning, Jack's bear suddenly decided he wanted to be far away. Jack fired instantly and scored a high lung shot as the bear was quartering away and downhill.

Blackie tumbled end over end and piled up in a dense clump of alders. We were so elated we didn't mind the inconvenience of the tangled brush. Time was running out for us, as a new party of hunters was due in camp the next day. Before morning the hide must be skinned, fleshed and salted so Jack and Dr. John could return to town on the plane that brought out the new party.

While we worked by the light of Coleman gas lanterns, Old Mel Horner, our cook, kept us supplied with coffee and cookies. Before midnight we were in bed, and the trophies were ready for the pack to the lake in the morning.

The hunt with the Seidenstickers was all but over. For me, in those few minutes before I yielded to sleep, the memories began. Dr. John could easily have downed that moose—a medium-sized bull and not far from camp. He had every legal right to it, but he knew the heavy back-packing and fleshing would work a hardship on the whole party, and his father might have had to forego his black bear hunting. "Don't believe my office is big enough to accommodate a rack like that!" Dr. John had said airily.

Such a fine hunt! We'd covered hundreds of miles together, hiked over and photographed some of the most spectacular scenery in the North. We'd counted more than 300 head of big game animals, and taken good trophies. All our rather complicated hunting plans had materialized without a hitch, and there'd been fishing as a bonus.

The sleeping bag felt wonderful in the frosty night air. The genuine regrets of parting with these two fine hunting companions would come with tomorrow—and the day would bring new hunters, new experiences, more trophies and no doubt more hard work. ■

We Like Mister Pike

Author, with fly rod, and Dixon, with spinning gear, connected with pike on the first casts and their lines threatened to cross.

By CHARLES J. KEIM
Photos by KEIM and JALBERT

Reprinted from Alaska Sportsman® , May, 1959 (ALASKA® magazine)

Current regulations specified that Alaska's great northern pike "may be taken at any time without regard to bag limits, and by use of a gill-net, trap, seine or spear in all waters of Alaska except in Unit 20 (Fairbanks-Central Tanana River area), where such taking shall be by hook, line or spear and in numbers according to the applicable bag limit."

Roland Jalbert, assistant professor of physics at the University of Alaska, and James Dixon, administrative assistant to the professor of military science and tactics, had that bag limit fixed firmly in their minds when we boarded Roland's four-place float-equipped plane one July and headed for Minto Lakes, 30 air miles west of Fairbanks, to catch some pike for our lockers.

During the previous summer, Roland and Jim and their wives had flown to the same place for the same purpose, unaware that the pike had been declared a game fish with a bag limit.

They had phenomenal luck and, with the usual pride of successful fishermen, when another plane arrived they signalled the occupants to come over and look at their catch. The two newcomers showed no interest, but the fishermen insisted. Reluctantly the two came over, and just as reluctantly they relieved the fishermen of their licenses for the year. They had exceeded the limit, and the visitors were enforcement agents.

Until 1957, when *Esox lucius*, the long, cavernous-mouthed great northern pike, was declared a game fish, few sportsmen even thought of trying to catch him on conventional tackle. They were too busy concentrating upon the rainbow, steelhead, cutthroat, Dolly Varden and mackinaw trout, the grayling and the salmon, all abundant in their Alaskan ranges. The inevitable result was that in waters easily accessible from cities and highways, these artistocratic species became somewhat less abundant.

When the law raised the social status of the great northern pike, sport fishermen decided to give him a go on light tackle. He put up such a tussle they've been going after him in increasing numbers ever since.

There's no mistaking the pike. He ranges from Bristol Bay north into the Arctic and eastward into Canada, but is absent from the Aleutian Islands, the southern coast and the Panhandle, and he's the sole member of the genus found in Alaska. Pike, pickerel and muskel-lunge are similar in shape, but the muskie's gill covers are bare, the pickerel's are heavily scaled, the pike's only partly scaled.

The present record for pike is 46 pounds and two ounces. But, according to Dr. Otto William Geist, paleontologist with the University of Alaska, far bigger ones have been caught by men interested in food, not records.

"One time," said Dr. Geist, who has spent much time in the range of the pike, "I saw a missionary and an Indian lugging a pike they'd taken in a large oxbow lake near Circle. Both men were medium-sized. They'd run a sapling through the pike's gills and were carrying the pole over their shoulders, and the pike's tail was dragging the ground."

As Roland's plane lifted us off the Chena River just below the university campus, I shouted jestingly above the roar of the motor, "What's the limit for pike this year in Wildlife Management Unit 20?"

Roland, just as jestingly, gave me a sour look and clamped on his ear phones to file a flight plan with the FAA at the Fairbanks International Airport. Jim grinned and in army fashion quoted the page and paragraph number of the regulations which stated, "ten fish daily or in possession: Provided, that except for northern pike such limit may not contain more than two fish over twenty inches in length."

Jim Dixon decides this pike is big enough to keep.

A medium-sized pike tested Dixon's skill and gear. Hooking a pike isn't always followed by landing it.

We climbed steadily for a while, then barrelled through the smoke of a large forest fire on some of the hills edging the valley in which the hundreds of lakes known as the Minto Lakes are nestled.

We'd fished the lakes successfully before, but this time we decided that, as pike prefer sloughs and backwaters, we'd try the confluence of silt-laden Goldstream Creek and a clear-water outlet from one of the larger lakes. Our landmark was a cluster of old caches where the Indians occasionally stretch their nets to catch pike. Hundreds of ducks and geese dotted the placid lakes as we flew low over them. The Minto area is one of the principal waterfowl breeding grounds in Interior Alaska.

We circled the fish camp once, then Roland skillfully set the plane down in a slough so narrow that the wing tips almost brushed the willows along both banks.

Roland and Jim assembled their spinning gear equipped with eight-pound monofilament, and I joined a medium-heavy glass fly rod with a light reel and twelve-pound-test nylon line. All of us tied large

110

red-and-white spoons to the light wire leaders, and that's all the gear we needed in one and one-half hours of fishing.

Not that we didn't lose some of it. Roland lost a spoon with his first cast. There was a swirl of water where his spoon went down, and even before he started to retrieve, a pike exploded into the air, danced on its tail, then bellied down into the water and kept right on going in the direction of the lake.

Jim and I didn't have time to commiserate with Roland, because each of us hooked a fighter on the first cast and we were busy playing tug-of-war.

Jim's spinning rod bent like a Toledo blade as he tried to check his pike's run toward my line.

"They're going to cross, Jim," I shouted. Jim, his cigarette clamped between his teeth like a cigar, merely nodded.

As the two lines almost converged, Jim's pike decided to try the air for a while, head snapping back and forth like a dog worrying an old shoe. My pike tried for depth and a run, and I had to take up fast by hand as he headed toward me. Then he did a 180, and my reel clicked like a hot Geiger counter. I finally slowed him as his runs grew shorter

Author starts cleaning part of the catch, which will go into cold storage for winter eating. His party had reason to remember the legal limit on this newly restricted game fish.

Dixon hands Jalbert another pike to load for the homeward flight. Weight and length of runway really set the limit of the catch.

and he went into a series of jumps and belly flops near shore. I took advantage of these to horse him onto the bank.

Two of my three hooks were buried in the pike's tough mouth, but I had to extract only one with the long-nosed pliers I used to avoid the ugly rows of sharp teeth in the huge maw. The second hook was sufficiently bent to pull almost straight out.

My pike weighed approximately 10 pounds. Jim's was smaller. He held it belly down in the water until it gathered up a little steam, then he turned it loose. Roland, meanwhile, had caught an eight- or nine-pounder.

112

While I photographed the two men fishing, another pike hit Roland's spoon, straightened out a number three large safety pin snap and kept right on going.

Roland muttered something I didn't quite catch, then borrowed one of my heavier wire leaders. He fastened it to a larger red-and-white spoon, scarred with the teeth of last year's pike, and spun the lure to the far bank. He had just started his retrieve when his arms and the rod jarred with the impact of a strike.

The pike ran upstream and down, submarined and jumped, but this time the tackle held. The pike weighed 27 pounds dressed when we returned to the campus.

We thought we'd take home our limits that day, and we could have done so if Roland had thought we could get off the water with our load. We switched to single hooks and turned loose our fighters after that. Even so, Roland had to ferry Jim and the fish over to the lake, then come back after me, and take off with the longer and straighter run of the lake.

When we cleaned the fish we found eight- and nine-inch pike inside the big ones, and I found what looked like the remains of a duck.

"I used to see pike take ducks near our dredging operations," said Dr. Ernest N. Patty, then president of the University of Alaska. "They reminded me of tigers. They would actually jump clear of the water and down on their prey. One of my employees had a favorite pike lure—a handful of feathers tied to a large hook."

No matter what the pike eats, it seems, he tastes good. Many Alaskans prefer to fillet the fish, strip off the yellowish-spotted, greenish-gray skin, roll the flesh in flour and fry it. The flesh draws back from the smaller bones during the frying, and they can be removed easily. The larger pike are also good cut in large chunks and boiled or baked.

The pike we caught on that July trip began tasting especially good when the snow started to fly and the lakes and streams were freezing over.

Not that we can't catch pike through the ice. That's a sport Alaskans discovered a long time ago, but it's another story, for another season.

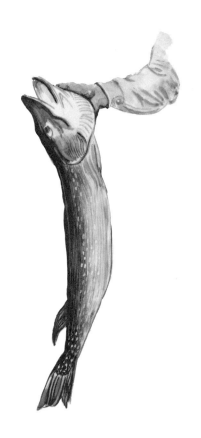

Pike – On Ice

I was proud of my pair.

By CHARLES J. KEIM

Reprinted from Alaska Sportsman® , January, 1960 (ALASKA® magazine)

For centuries Alaskan Natives have patiently chopped holes in the ice, fitted a line with a lure and jigged it up and down to catch fish.

Today increasing numbers of latter-day Alaskans are taking the cue from their Native brethren and with perhaps flashier but no more effective gear are supplementing their winter routines with genuine sport and their rations with fresh fish.

That's what three of us from the University of Alaska did one February when a brief but sunshiny Sunday free from examination paper correcting beckoned us to the boondocks. Our trio consisted of Roland Jalbert, physics prof and pilot; Donald Peterson, Alaskan teacher and my friend from Montana, and this writer.

Our "just-in-case" emergency gear, including sleeping bags, took up the last seat in Roland's four-place plane as we headed west of Fairbanks into the vast bowl in which are located the hundreds of Minto Lakes.

Roland caught the first fat pike.

Don drew first shift on the ice spud.

We were after Great Northern Pike because those we'd caught on light gear the previous summer and fall were gone from our deep freezers. And we'd learned long before they officially became a game fish two years ago that they are scrappy fighters and good food.

We worked after Roland effortlessly set down his ski-equipped plane on a large and snow-covered lake. First we shoveled away the snow, then with a heavy and sharp spud chipped through about 30 inches of ice. We started with big hole outlines, but as the depth of the holes increased we were quite willing to let them take a funnel form until about a half-hour later the spud pierced the remaining shells of ice, and cold, clear water welled up to the level of the frozen lake surface.

An airplane covers ground better than a dog team.

We purposely let our pike partially freeze for easier filleting at home.

Don gingerly drew in a lightly hooked Northern.

We used telescoped metal fish poles, strong cutty-hunk line and large red-and-white lures at the end of a wire leader. We tossed the lures into the holes right after we chipped them because we'd learned earlier that the pounding and sunlight seem to attract the big ones who won't hang around long.

The technique paid off with fighting fish longer than the holes were deep, as the accompanying photographs show. We didn't mind that our hands became a bit cold at times and the water froze on the lines and line guides. After all, that same cold was freezing the many pike we caught and they'd be just right for easy filleting when we returned home for another week of classes and with pleasant memories of pike jigging in the sub-Arctic. ■

Mixed Bag

We found the black at the end of his bouncy trail. He was well-furred, prime and powerfully built.

Story and photos by HAL WAUGH

Reprinted from Alaska Sportsman® , September, 1959 (ALASKA® magazine)

Disconsolately I stared through the tent flap at some of the finest hunting range in all Alaska. We were camped on the South Fork of the Kuskokwim, a glacial stream originating in the Alaska Range. Its maze of silty channels crossed and recrossed, giving it a braided effect.

This was to be a real back beyond 21-day mixed hunt in an unexcelled area. Somewhere up there, grazing on the hillside, was a fine ram with a full curl that J. R. Baker meant to hang on his wall back in Donophin, Missouri.

The ram was there, all right, but we were in the valley and J. R. had a lame knee.

121

"Why did this have to happen to me?" I groaned to Fleming Clemson, my packer and friend of long standing. The old-timers that J. R. had come for, the ones with trophy heads, stayed in the remote areas where man's foot seldom steps. Knees had to be in good working order to cross the muskegs, reach the foothills and climb above timberline. At least, Fleming and I thought so.

"Maybe it won't last long," Fleming said hopefully. "A little liniment might fix it right up."

Mentally I rummaged through my possible bag for liniment. Some people had faith in its healing properties. We used to use it on horses.

J. R., in his early fifties, was a real estate broker in his work-a-day life, a hunter by avocation. It was up to me to show him the kind of trophies he was here for. He was to show me something before the hunt was over.

The weather was friendly next day. Feverishly, in our desire to be off and away, we did our routine camp chores. We'd pack over to one of my spike camps, a sure-fire location for sheep, sometimes grizzlies, and a few black bears.

Fleming and I carried the bare essentials of food, sleeping bags, camera and ammunition. J. R. hobbled along beside us. High on a mountain slope, looking closer in the clear atmosphere than it really was, I spotted a band of grazing sheep. They looked like scattered white boulders or tiny snow patches. J. R. raised his glasses.

"Thirty of them!" he cried.

"Ewes and lambs," I told him, "and a few immature rams. We keep them there to whet your appetite. Tomorrow we'll have you up on top where the old gents hang out."

As the day wore on we skirted the shore of a small lake, climbed a ridge and stopped for a rest. With binoculars we watched a distant grizzly dig for mice. After another short hike we settled down for lunch and a midday nap.

"Couldn't have slept sounder in my own bed," J. R. said as we began stirring.

"It's part of the daily treatment," I told him. "Some hunters don't want to bother with it at first. They come to hunt, not waste time sleeping on a mountain. Before long, though, after the city blood thins down, they're the first ones down and the last ones up."

On reaching the spike camp we erected the crawl-in type tents and lean-to. Fleming and I shared one tent. J. R. took the other. We were content to roll into our sleeping bags early, after a hasty meal.

Night sounds took over the mountains. Some time later, while a procession of disjointed thoughts and visions was going through my mind, Fleming reached over and poked me. I lay still, trying to bring myself back to reality.

Something was thumping through the willow brush within feet of the tent. There was a snuffling, a snorting, with a breathiness to it. Brush cracked as this noisy creature worked from the side of the tent around to the back. With the continuing breathiness there was a menacing growl.

"A grizzly," I whispered.

I made no move. Grizzlies mind their own business—or do they? My skin tingled as I remembered pictures I'd seen proving that they don't always. Several years ago a Fish and Wildlife Service stream guard shot a brownie from his sleeping bag. He dropped it half in and half out of his tent door.

"When he identifies the man scent he'll go away," I whispered with faint conviction. "I'd hate to try shooting a bear in this darkness. Besides, the season isn't open."

Minutes dragged on. The bear didn't go away. There were minor crashes, loud in the night air, and the gurgling growl continued. Evidently he was trying to get at our food supply.

Finally I unzipped my bag, fumbled about for some tin pans, and handed them to Fleming. I found some more for myself, and we set up a barrage of pan rattling and loud talking that should have scared any bear over the next ridge. We paused and strained our ears. The bear was still there.

Shivering, we slipped back into our bags, but we were not to sleep for awhile. We tried once more, unsuccessfully, to scare off our visitor. He left when it suited him.

"How did you like having a bear in camp in the middle of the night?" I asked J. R. by way of a good morning.

"What bear?" he demanded. We had to show him tracks to prove we weren't kidding.

Bacon, eggs, hot cakes and coffee cooked over the open fire finished waking us. We were out of camp as soon as it was light enough to shoot. Our route led around the mountain. We gained altitude steadily, all the while keeping a sharp lookout for rams. Each time we paused to rest we used the binoculars.

The fork of the river downstream was the location of an early day roadhouse. Spring torrents and under-cuttings have swept the remains away. The old trail was a link between Cook Inlet and the waters of the Kuskokwim, which flows into Bristol Bay. A lot of history is locked in this uninhabited area.

It is wonderful country for sheep—few hunters, and only a smattering of wolves.

"There are two up there waiting for us," I said, "just below the rock cliff."

J. R. swung his glasses about. "How good are they?" he asked hopefully.

"Can't tell much from here, but my guess is at least one has a full curl. More likely both of them. Can you make it up there to claim one?"

"No reason why not," he answered testily. "What are we waiting for?"

Before we could start our ascent we had to go downhill, cross the drainage, and pick our way precariously up the slope diagonally to the feeding sheep. They would be out of our view, but with a normal amount of speed and good luck we could come out above them in a couple of hours. I had taken rams on this mountain before, and could eliminate time-consuming digressions. Sheep aren't particularly fickle. They'd stay around for a while.

Using brush and convenient boulders, we moved steadily until we arrived at a point that should have put the rams below us. Snaking along on my stomach, I raised my hand in warning as I caught sight of the two beautiful creatures placidly lying down surveying the country below.

J. R. was right beside me. "You're in luck," I whispered, lowering my glasses. "They're both full curl. I think the horn is broomed on the . . ."

124

Before I could finish, a dislodged rock had both rams on their feet. One to the left, one to the right, they broke into their characteristic bouncy run.

J. R. fired two quick shots from his Remington '06. The ram on the right collapsed, while his confused partner halted and stood broadside to us. He couldn't figure out what was happening in his little world. I tossed a rock at him and told him to be on his way, forever wary of man.

"You've got yourself a dandy Dall," I told J. R. over the carcass. "When you see that full curl head-dress on the wall of your trophy room back home, you can remember this windswept peak with the rain beating down on three chilly mortals, struggling to get off the mountain. Smell the rain in the air?"

"I'll remember a lot of things," J. R. retorted, "but mostly I want to remember how good the chops taste. You boys don't have to keep me on a perpetual diet. When do we eat?"

The rain began to fall. It increased steadily while Fleming and I did a hurry-up job of fleshing, quartering and pack-lashing. The

The ram was there, all right, and J. R. went up to claim him. Fleming was along to help carry him down.

mountaintop is an awesome place at any time, and particularly during an August rainstorm. The thought of camp appealed to us all.

We'd filled only part of J. R.'s bag. He was to remind us of it sooner than we expected, considering that bum knee he might have nursed for a few days back in the main camp.

"Don't think I don't appreciate this good fishing and your fine company, boys," he goaded, "but if it's all the same to you, I'd rather have it out yonder somewhere. You've pacified me with steaks, chops, grayling, spruce grouse and ptarmigan, fried, roasted, broiled and boiled. But what about my moose? Where's my caribou? My grizzly?"

"You have a point, J. R.," I told him, "but I have to admit your moose and caribou orders can't be filled—not right now. The mild weather has worked against us. They won't come out of the high country while it's mild. The grizzly is a different proposition. He's around, but the opening day isn't."

For several days I had deliberately kept our party out of the hills surrounding camp, to keep from scaring off any of the wily, highly intelligent grizzlies. They were not fair game until September first. We had seen a few moose and caribou, but the outsized old bulls just weren't around. They were back in the hills and canyons. The rut would be slow to get under way. Better trophy hunting doesn't come until the bulls collect in the lower valleys, and the hunter has a chance at numbers rather than solitary bulls.

Fall shades of yellows, reds, greens and browns blended into a riot of colors. Sharply etched mountain peaks pierced the clear blue of the Interior skies. Puffy white clouds drifted by. We set out one brisk morning to find a high knoll with a view of the muskeg flats, the timbered expanses and the surrounding hills. It was a tough climb for all of us, but J. R. stayed right with us. He wanted a grizzly, and no trick knee was going to stop him.

We looked for a grizzly. We were always looking for a grizzly. All about us was an abundance of feed, and sufficient cover to please the most discriminating of animals. A gentle breeze was coming down the mountainside. It was hard country to hunt, but on this day a certain male grizzly was to use up his luck.

When we first saw him he looked like a dark ball rolling through the brush. He stopped here and there at an especially appealing berry patch, then rolled on. I looked at J. R. His face appeared to puff out in eager anticipation.

"He's a beauty," I told him, "a regular mountain grizzly. They sleep too long to grow very big. The climate is against them. There's no telling what a bear will do, so we'll have to get right after him. Stay right with me, and when I tell you to shoot, be sure you take your time and make it good."

Veering to the left, we followed low on the side of a ridge. After covering about a hundred yards, we stopped and noted that the bear had stopped too. Evidently he planned to bed down right in our line of approach—unusual luck!

"Take him!" I whispered.

J. R. fired. The impact lofted the bear sidewise. He lay with all four feet pointing toward us, like a dog asleep on his side. J. R., so jubilant he forgot all about his bad leg, was on his feet dancing a jig with the exuberance of a kid. That's when the bear flipped, and in the next instant he was gone.

I scrambled up the ridge to the spot where the bear had fallen. "He's hit hard," I told J. R. when he joined me. "See the blood? I don't think he's gone far . . . There!" I pointed to a patch of brush about seventy yards away.

J. R. fired and the bear disappeared again. There was silence. A bird flitted from a nearby bush. Somewhere, far off, a raven called. Somewhere, close by, was a wounded grizzly. I motioned J. R. to move beside me but several feet away, and we made our way to the spot where I'd seen the bear disappear.

"Stay here and cover me," I said. "I'm going down." He looked as if he wanted to give me an argument, then, realizing it was better this way, nodded.

Inching my way through the brush, I checked my safety. The hair on my head raised a bit. Every year, somewhere along the line, I managed to find myself in a hair-raiser like this. Cautiously I picked my way, all senses alert.

Several yards farther on, I spotted a dark heap. It was J. R.'s grizzly, dead as yesterday's cigar ash. J. R. limped up, and we sat down for a smoke. There was lots of time now to look him over, admire him, examine the wounds for bullet damage. How he managed to move after the first shot is a wonder, for his wound was at the top of his neck just in front of the hump, and included the spinal column. The second shot had caught him in the brain.

Again J. R. was as jubilant as a sourdough who'd found two nuggets in his pan. But like that sourdough, who wanted more gold for his poke, J. R. wanted more game for his bag. But the days were passing all too quickly. For three mornings we'd found ice in the water bucket.

We kept on a vigilant search for a trophy moose and caribou bulls, enjoyed watching bands of grazing sheep, were entertained by an old cow moose that forced me to shinny up a cache, and watched a feeding grizzly.

"Sure wish he was a big old blackie," J. R. was muttering to anyone who would listen. He was putting the final touches on a mess of grayling he'd caught in the beautiful little mountain lake at base camp.

"Blackies don't reach longevity in this country," I told him. "Too many grizzlies. When we do find a gambler, he's glossy black and nice. Let's concentrate on blackies these last few days. Then if a big bull moose bothers us, we'll take him too."

J. R. grinned. He really wanted a black to go with that fine grizzly. I had hopes, but we'd really have to hunt for it.

As we traveled north on a game trail that gradually led us high onto a mountain, we paused frequently to look for blackies. We'd done the same thing the day before, but succeeded only in getting a good workout. Today we had an added pair of sharp eyes, for Larry Keeler was with us as packer. Larry has the kind of imperturbability about him that's needed in school bus drivers or country mail carriers.

I was prepared for Larry's casual observation when he drawled, "There's a blackie in the berry brush beyond the slide."

I picked him up immediately. The wind was in our favor, and the bear was far enough away for us to make a good approach. One thing was for sure—J. R. would have to get on the move, bad leg or no. Blackies in this country are where you get them, not where you first see them.

"He'll disappear as fast as a paycheck," I told J. R. as I strode off, leaving him to keep up as best he could. Larry came along behind. We

A beautiful little mountain lake at base camp yielded grayling. This is a hunting area unexcelled over the last fifty years.

had a fair cover of brush. Sooner than I expected, the bear appeared on a little finger ridge, ambling downhill, broadside to us. I ducked low and waited for J. R. to come in close. Any vagrant breeze would send our quarry scurrying for brushier parts. I signaled to J. R. to shoot. It seemed interminably long before I saw the black tumble forward end over end, and heard the crack of the gun.

"Hit him again!" I shouted, and J. R. squeezed off the second shot. The bullet struck the dirt. The bear tumbled on. J. R. connected with the third shot, and I felt reasonably sure no bear would reach the valley floor and take off after all this one was going through.

We started down and found him dead at the end of the bouncy trail. He needed some cleaning up, but he was a well-furred, prime, and a powerfully built animal.

"When I quit learning, I'll quit guiding," I said when J. R. hobbled up. "You and blackie, here, have taught me another lesson." I held out the bear's right foreleg. "This leg's been broken and healed over. He's got a bulky, stiff elbow, but he was getting around okay and I didn't notice anything abnormal about his gait."

"And how do I fit in?"

"Well," I admitted, "when I saw that limp of yours, I was plenty worried about how you were going to get around to bag your ram, and your grizzly, and blackie here."

J. R. snorted his disgust while Larry and I skinned the blackie and packed the skin back to camp. He told me then, and he has told me at intervals since, that no knee was going to hold him back from a hunt—and it hasn't. He was back the next year for his moose and caribou, and when, after hunting in Idaho, Mexico, Spitzbergen and Colombia, South America, he got ready to go to Africa, he took me along. He wasn't worrying about the knee, he explained, but he wanted his African trophies to measure up to those he got in Alaska. ■

King Of The Chetaslina

All hands work on the landing strip, key to Hal's valley and the coming hunt.

Story and photos by CHARLES J. KEIM

Reprinted from Alaska Sportsman®, October, 1962 (ALASKA® magazine)

"That's the valley, Chuck. You people ought to find a grizzly there, maybe the old one."

Jack Wilson, veteran Alaska bush pilot, shouted above the roar of his Piper Family Cruiser and then pointed. For a moment I almost forgot I was in the plane.

To our right magnificent Mt. Wrangell thrust up its 14,005-foot peak. The almost dormant fires beneath the ancient volcano painted the perpetual feather of steam and smoke across a blue and otherwise clear sky. Tremendous masses of jumbled ice and snow formed into glaciers farther down the slopes, and one, Chetaslina Glacier, entered the head of the valley. From this glacier's terminus tumbled the angry, milk colored Chetaslina River. I looked left; the stream raged for miles down the valley to drain into the mighty Copper River which ultimately empties into tidewater another 90 miles away.

131

Lost in wonderment at the view, I scarcely noticed that Jack was guiding the plane downward. Then I looked for the landing strip and couldn't find it. Jack did. The plane bumped over part of the rocky, willow dotted bank alongside the turbulent stream, and the bumps didn't stop until the plane did, almost at the water's edge.

"She came down okay, but she didn't want to stop," imperturbable Jack commented. Then we unhooked our safety harnesses from our shoulders and laps and climbed out of the plane to meet Hal Waugh who would be guiding the party that was forming for a 1959 grizzly hunt in the Wrangell mountains near the Yukon Territory and at the start of the 49th state's panhandle.

"Still plague-taked bumpy," Hal said, the perpetual grin sweeping more widely across his ruggedly handsome face. It was a typical comment, for Alaskans and others identify Hal by his "plague take" comments as surely as they label him one of the top guides in the north country.

We unloaded the plane and as Jack headed back to Chitina for more gear Hal introduced me to Andy Runyan. He had set up base camp and would be guiding another of Hal's clients, Wade Martin of Pennsylvania. Jack would bring him in the next day.

The introductions over, we headed back to the river bank where Dale Miller of Valdez, Alaska, still was busily tossing aside the larger granite and lava boulders and cutting down willows. He'd help Hal as a packer on the hunt which would start in a few days when Dr. and Mrs Robert V. Broadbent of Reno, Nevada, would show up. In the meantime we'd all work on the strip which really was the key to Hal's valley and the hunt itself.

Hal pridefully had told me about the valley while he was attending summer session at the University of Alaska.

"I've scouted that area from the air for five years to find a place I figured we could set down a plane and, more importantly, get it back into the air," Hal had explained. "As nearly as I can tell, no one has hunted the valley for a half century, although a couple of trappers do have a cabin there which they haven't used for a number of years. I finally found a place where Jack could land and take off, and I hired an old trapper to pack in and help clear off some of the brush and

Left—Author examines parts of the porch. It had been a fine cabin, but was the old grizzly suitably avenged for the long-lasting pain in his mouth? Right—At the spike camp, six miles farther up the Chetaslina, grizzlies, blacks, rams and moose were near at hand but still the river seemed bent on shielding them.

rocks to make it a little safer. Why don't you come in at the end of the summer session at the university?"

So there we were—clearing the strip to make it safer for the plane when it would bring in Bob and Kay and would be more heavily loaded at the end of the hunt with passengers and gear and, we hoped, the M.D.'s trophies.

"Take a look at that," Hal said that first evening while scanning the hillsides above our valley and across the Chetaslina.

For a long time we watched a large, golden-brown grizzly sow and her twin cubs feed on the blueberries which grew in profusion and which had also constituted our supper dessert.

"Good sign," we all agreed, then as darkness fell we sat around the cook tent drinking coffee and talking about the big bear Jack had referred to when we first flew into the valley. The two trappers had mentioned the big one almost every time they'd returned to Chitina for supplies or to end their season of trapping.

"He's always around, looking things over, snooping into everything, but wary enough to keep clear of us," they'd say. "We've tried to get him, but he's cagey, even more than most grizzlies, and that's saying something."

Jack flew Wade Martin in next day in a Supercub plane. Then he lifted the plane back into the air after a run of 47 paces, and we all worked hard on the strip. A piece of plastic fastened to a high pole served as a wind sock, and we used five-gallon gas cans and pieces of cloth to mark both borders of the strip which wound somewhat crookedly around the river bank. The sow and her cubs continued to feed on the berries and serve as the chief topic of conversation until we visited the trappers' cabin.

"I looked over the cabin last June when we first hazarded a landing in here," Hal explained as we walked along an old trail. "The cabin's still in pretty good shape and . . . " He stopped as we topped a small rise, then let out a low whistle of amazement.

"Look at that plague taked mess!"

The four walls and the roof of the cabin were, indeed, quite intact, but the log porch, the grill of heavy logs which had been chained and nailed over the door, and the door itself were in shambles. The inside of the cabin looked like some giant had gone to work with a tremendous eggbeater. Matches, cartridges, tools, clothing and dozens of other articles were strewn from the back inside wall of the cabin to the outside path leading to the structure.

"A grizzly, no doubt about it," Hal said as he plucked several pinches of long, brownish-yellow hair from the doorway and some of the logs. We found more of the same hair adhering to the resin which had oozed from relatively fresh tooth and claw slashes on many spruce trees about the cabin.

"That plague taked bear doesn't like people, or wants to show who's king around here," Hal said as we viewed the shambles. "He wasn't just looking for food. What a mess."

We had plenty of time to speculate as to whether or not this was the work of "the big one" because the warm, clear weather changed quickly to wind and rain which kept Bob and Kay grounded in Chitina for two days, although once Jack circled camp with his two passengers, then, just before attempting a landing, decided against it.

"Well, we know they'll be coming in," Hal said. "Dale, how about getting us some camp meat?"

Dale unlimbered his .375 Winchester magnum and headed upstream. He returned late that evening quite wet, but with a triumphant grin on his face.

"Got our meat on my license," he announced. "A nice bull moose, about a mile above camp and across the Chetaslina."

He'd found a place where the river braided out in several channels, then had waded across to dress out the moose.

"Good thing I got him early in the morning before the rain, combined with the glacier meltoff, had caused the stream to go way up," Dale added. "As it was, I found it a little tough to get back across the river."

Early next morning Dale, Andy and I trudged upriver to haul back the meat. We made it across a braided out section of the river after considerable effort. When close to shore I slipped on a rock, lost my footing and was rolled to shore by the current. While I wiped some moisture from my camera which I'd strapped near my neck, Andy broke what he called "Indian kerosene" or dead spruce boughs from trees and built a large fire by which we all warmed ourselves. Then we tied meat on our packboards, hung the remainder high in a spruce and tried to cross the river.

Andy tied around his waist a nylon cord I'd packed along. Then he stepped out into the river which visibly had risen while we had worked. Dale and I held onto the cord and slowly paid it out. For a time, the weight of the meat on Andy's back gave him pretty good footing. Then, as the water caught his load, he began to lose footing and balance. Finally he stumbled back to us.

We headed downstream, unsuccessfully trying again and again to cross at points where the current seemingly slowed and the water shallowed. In the more turbulent sections we could hear the grinding of huge boulders as they rolled downstream. And always the river crept higher, for by now the sun was illuminating the valley above us and shining brightly and warmly upon the glacier which was the source of the stream.

When we were almost opposite camp, Andy signalled Hal and Wade with his .44 magnum revolver. The two men quickly sized up the

Left—"He must be mighty tall!" Hal said as he and Dale (at left) looked at the remains of the cloth we had hung over the meat on the crosspole. Right—Jack, dropping in to see how the hunt was going, takes Hal's and Kay's letters. This time, too, there were sheep horns and capes to take out.

situation, brought a long rope from camp and pointed upstream to a less wild stretch.

There was no use shouting. We worked by signals. Wade, quite a baseball player back in Pennsylvania, tied one end of the rope to a rock and with a mighty whirl slung it across the river. We tied the nylon cord to it and with this lengthened rope we see-sawed our watches, rifles, binoculars and my camera across to Hal and Wade, all of us taking great care to hold the rope above the cold, watery haystacks.

"Well, we get wet, even if our gear didn't," Andy said. We tied the rope under his arms and pack and he carefully stepped into the current. When it threw him, Hal and Wade pulled him ashore. I was next, and got just as wet and cold.

Dale was last. When he finally stumbled, the cold water caused him to shout what he later said was "Oh!"

We all misunderstood the word and began to pull all the harder, submarining Dale who really wanted us to hold steady on the rope until he could gain some semblance of footing. So he traveled underwater to reach shore, and around hot coffee in the cook tent that afternoon and thereafter his "Oh" was cause for merriment that Dale took in good humor.

Andy and I tied the hard-earned meat high on a crosspole and we served Bob and Kay fresh moose liver when Jack flew the young couple into base camp.

We didn't stay in camp long. Both Bob and Wade wanted a Dall sheep, so Andy and Wade headed for the peaks behind the camp and the rest of us hiked six miles toward Mt. Wrangell and a spike camp Dale and Andy had set up the day after our arrival.

Next morning the rain, which had soaked us thoroughly during our hike, was gone. For a time the sun rolled along the rim of the mountain towering above spike camp then flooded the upper reaches of the valley. A light breeze scudded the few clouds from the sky until only the perpetual steam cloud issuing from Mt. Wrangell remained.

"Hey, it's great to be alive," Hal said, and the fragrance of the coffee he'd made drifted past our faces which were protruding from the sleeping bags. Before we could crawl from their warmth Hal had served us coffee and a cigarette, and though we grumbled at this deluxe service thoroughly enjoyed it.

"Let's get a sheep, Bob," Hal called as Bob and Kay emerged from their small tent.

"I'm game," Bob replied, and made the French toast which we downed with bacon and coffee before Dale headed downriver to bring up a moose quarter and Hal, Bob, Kay and I moved upriver in search of the Dalls.

"Fresh grizzly, blackie and moose sign." Hal pointed to a mixture of tracks in the moist sand along the river. All appeared to be heading toward the glacier which awesomely loomed ahead, its terminus a jumbled mass of ice streaked with boulders, soil and other detritus it had picked up in its inexorable movement down the slopes of Mt. Wrangell.

"I'd like to head after those bear, Hal," Bob said. "Wish the bear season still wasn't several days away."

"So do I," Hal replied, "but we'll have to get our sheep now. We'll have plenty of time for bear. Besides, let's sort of hold out for the King of the Chetaslina. He's down there somewhere, and I'd like to see you get him."

Bob, who is built like a medium sized Notre Dame fullback, nodded his crewcut head in agreement, shifted the pack he'd asked to carry, and helped Kay jump her 114 pounds across a small cut the river had made in the bank. Then we all sat down on some of the water smoothed boulders and glassed a mountain to the right of the glacier and approximately three-quarters of a mile away.

"There are five Dalls," Hal said, then adjusted his tripod-mounted spotting 'scope to a finer focus. "They're all full curl rams."

We all looked at the sheep, three of which were lying down on a lichen covered slope below a ragged overhang of rimrocks. The other two were standing and looking over the vast bowl below them. Even from our distance the 'scope showed us that the horns of one of these animals flared out magnificently from the full curl.

"That's the one we want," Hal said. He led us across three almost hip deep river braids and then up the steep side of a gully which hid us from the Dalls' sharp eyes. Hal and Bob made the final sneak which would place them a little above the animals.

Kay and I caught our breath, then toiled upward at Hal's disappointed beckon.

"Gone. I'll be plague taked if I know where."

This same pattern repeated for several days, during which we counted more than 200 of the especially wary animals. They always were high above us and across the river.

Finally on the sixth day of the hunt when I remained in camp the others returned with a superb, full curl Dall. Bob had dropped it right next to the Chetaslina Glacier with a 250-yard shot in the rib cage using a 150-grain Nosler bullet in his Saturn .30-06 ICL mounted with a Pecar four-power 'scope.

Bob was elated with his trophy which rough camp measurements put at 161½ points. Over hot coffee and moose stew we talked about the stalk he'd made. Then the talk shifted to five grizzlies and the blackie the party had spotted that day, but had bypassed because the season still was closed.

"One grizzly ran approximately two miles up the slope when he finally scented us," Bob said. "I've never seen such stamina."

Hal was equally enthusiastic about the largest grizzly they'd seen.

"His color reminded me of the sunflowers I've seen while living in Idaho, and he was big, too. Well, we'll head back to base camp tomorrow and if we can't locate the King after a reasonable time, we'll come back up here and look for Sunflower."

We were elated but tired when we reached base camp next day. Smoke was rising from the cook tent smoke pipe, and Andy and Wade greeted us with welcome cups of hot coffee.

"I got a Dall," Andy said. He pointed to the horns and cape which he and Wade had placed at the base of a huge tree in front of the cook tent. That year it was legal for a guide to hunt, too.

"Guess you and I should have hiked the moose meat right up to the top of that tree, Chuck," Andy said. "A grizzly stole it while we were all gone. Must have winded the meat when he was just about to push down Bob's and Kay's tent."

We followed Andy to the meat pole. It was only a pole now. The meat was gone, all of it. Not a chunk or bone of almost three-quarters of the moose remained. Frayed ropes dangled from the pole. Below it we found the tattered remnants of the ground cloth we'd hung above the meat to protect it from the rain.

Hal ruefully sized up the situation then examined the trees which supported the pole. He removed several tufts of hair adhering to the rough bark.

"It's the same plague taked hair we found at the cabin. That critter must have stood on his hind legs and jumped like an Olympic champ, and even then he'd had to have been mighty tall."

We compared the hair with that we'd found near the wrecked cabin, and the tufts were alike. Then we looked at Bob's and Kay's tent. The bear had stood at the back and apparently had merely leaned his forepaws against it before he'd scented the meat. Even such a casual gesture, however, had been sufficient to bend the tubular tent frame out of line and caused his claws to pierce the canvas.

"Had another visitor in camp this morning, too," Andy explained. "He was a blackie, big one, evidently coming around for the leavings. I almost bumped into him as I walked out of the cook tent. He rared up and stared at me. I stared back from about 10 feet. I drew my .44 magnum just in case, and blackie skedaddled back into the woods. He should have stuck around. Wade still was in his sleeping bag; I'd have invited blackie in for hotcakes and coffee."

Andy was in pretty high spirits. While we had been out in the spike camps Jack Wilson had flown in with some mail which had informed

Andy that his first child, a girl, had arrived at Juneau and that his wife was okay.

"My wife says that the baby weighs nine pounds and is 21 inches long," Andy said, then added, "No record, but good average."

"Well, Bob, maybe you'll be able to use that blackie tag you've been packing," Hal said as we sat around the coffee pot after we'd surveyed the damage. "We'll try for King first though."

Hal wasn't vindictive just because the King had paid us a visit while we weren't home and hadn't been a very friendly guest. Bob wanted a grizzly, and that was that. Actually, Hal likes bears, and I've yet to encounter an Alaskan guide who respects and knows them more. He has gained that knowledge during 35 years of hunting them and has built a reputation for producing them for his clients. He guided a client to the fourth largest brownie on record and the largest ever recorded by a non-resident.

Bear season was to open the next day, September 1, and summer abruptly changed into fall that night. Hal swished ice around in the coffee pot when the camp began stirring. Mt. Wrangell and the other peaks right down the ladder to our camp had new snow covers. After the frost disappeared in the bright sun we noticed for the first time that the blueberry and other bushes on the surrounding hills were trying to match color for color the rainbows that had followed the frequent showers.

Andy and Wade headed for our spike camp. While Dale and I worked around camp, Hal and Bob hunted upstream for the King.

The gallon and one-half coffee pot was boiling and the Dall sheep steaks cut and ready for frying when Hal and Bob returned mighty late because they were packing a blackie hide that squared out 6' ½" before fleshing and 6' 3½" afterwards.

"We were hunting one of the ridges paralleling the Chetaslina," Bob explained. "I'd just turned down a moose that Hal estimated had over a 50-inch rack. I didn't want to risk spooking any bear that might be around, particularly if it were the King. Then we spotted the blackie moseying along the river—of course it had to be the other side, about 300 yards away. I fired from a sitting position and literally broke his heart with a 150-grain Nosler bullet. Then . . . "

140

Bob and Kay cross a small creek feeding the Chetaslina. Mount Wrangell in the background.

" . . . you had to get across the river and back, and that's why you are wet to the shoulder blades," Kay cut in with a smile. She gave Bob a victory kiss, then handed him a cup of coffee. For dessert that night we had blueberry cobbler Kay had baked in the oven of the Yukon stove.

"Plague take it, but that's good," Hal said and looked hopefully and successfully at the other pan of cobbler.

"If Bob gets the King, I'll coax some pies out of that oven," Kay promised.

"Well, we'll sure try," Hal countered. "I kind of think that any grizzly should rate some pies. Of course, if we do get one, it'll probably be on the opposite side of the river, too, and I hate to think about getting a hide and skull that large across that plague taked stream."

Two days of hard hunting upriver produced bear sign of all sorts for Hal and Bob, including large footprints in the sand, but they all were old. Then on the third morning while an awakening sun chased off the snow which had visited the hills near camp, Hal suggested that the hunt shift to downriver.

"Maybe we'll pick up some fresh sign there," Hal said. "The King packed off a plague taked amount of eating material when he got our moose, and while it's gone by this time, he's going to remember that the pickings were kind of nice in this neck of the woods. Let's find him."

As things turned out, the King found us.

Approximately one mile below camp we found the first promising sign—a set of huge grizzly footprints trailing through a bed of sand which had washed into a bowl-like depression sufficiently close to the torrent to receive a wash of water at times when the river was highest.

"Only a couple of days old," Hal said. "Otherwise, the river would have washed them away when we had sun all day to work on the glacier and send the water up. This place looks promising."

Hal repeated that statement a little later when, after carefully glassing the river bed, the banks and the hillsides, we moved through patches of brush which fingered down the right bank and into the stream bed where only the hardiest brush survived. Again we found the tracks, and this time long, shallow trenches where the animal had dug for roots and, finding them, had pulled them ropelike upward through the sand.

"Can't tell if it's the King," Hal said. "But he's mighty big. Chuck, try putting your size 12 shoepacs into that track."

The fit was pretty close, except that my toes weren't quite wide enough, and my toenails needed to extend a few inches out of my shoepacs.

By 11 o'clock that morning we had worked approximately two miles downriver. Then we had to make a choice. Not much further downstream the water narrowed for a distance between high banks. We would have to perform careful footwork if we wanted to remain along the river, and if we'd climb the steep bank we'd have to keep going until we'd get through the brush and trees and hit the high ridge paralleling the stream.

We sat down to rest.

"We've found the sign on the river and though it has given us a bad time in the past, I think that we'll stick with it," Hal said. "The bear that has made that sign might not be the King, but he's king hereabouts. Notice that we haven't seen any wildlife down here? He has chased it out and has been feeding on berries and roots and the like—maybe our moose, too."

Then Hal performed two actions that brought the King to us. First, while we rested, he climbed the banks and briefly scouted the country behind us.

"A heavily wooded sort of draw," Hal announced when he returned a few minutes later. We whispered back and forth then. Hal remained silent, hunkered down on one knee next to me and constantly scanning the country.

"Don't move!"

Hal's tensely whispered words reached all of us, spread out in perhaps a 14-foot line. At the same time he shrugged his .308 Model '98 full stocked Mauser off his shoulder through his bent arm and into his hand, the weapon all the while remaining vertical and next to his body.

Just for a instant we saw the grizzly. He walked to the edge of the river bank and silhouetted his massive bulk against the skyline by rearing upward without pausing, gracefully twisting around and reversing direction. Just like that. No lost motion, no frantic hurry, no pause and no time for Bob to get more than halfway to his shoulder his rifle which he had laid down for an instant.

For as brief a time as the bear had shown himself Hal buried his face in his hands—no "plague take its," no words at all.

"My rustling around up there got him curious. Chuck, you and Kay stay here. Bob. Dale. Let's go. Fast and quiet; watch the wind, and careful in the brush."

Kay and I moved over to a large spruce that had withstood the flood action of the river and watched the three men carefully scrabble up the river bank. We waited then, expectantly and wordlessly—three minutes, five, seven.

Crack!

Bob's gun, we guessed.

Another wait.

Dale appeared on the skyline as had the grizzly.

"Got him," he called, and told us how as we walked toward the bear.

"We really searched the little draw behind us. Didn't see a thing. We were almost ready to give up when I decided to turn around and take a final look as a sort of clearing. Then I saw the bear. He was carefully moving, almost sneaking up the side of the draw approximately 60 yards away. I signalled fast to Hal and Bob because in a few more yards the bear would have been over the crown of the draw and out of sight.

"Bob just plopped down into a sitting position, sighted his rifle for an instant and let off. The bear, and he's the King for sure, lurched forward a couple of steps and that was that."

Hal waited for a time after we joined him and Bob. Then he carefully circled above the inert bulk of the grizzly and finally touched his rifle, which he was holding pistol-like, against the back of the bear's neck. A few jabs. No movement.

"Come on up and look at the King you dethroned, Bob," Hal called.

We skinned him then. He had the same distinctive hair we'd found at the cabin and our meat pole. Bob's 150-grain Nosler had penetrated behind the shoulder, angled into and through the heart and lodged in a rib on the opposite side.

"A beautiful shot, Bob," Hal said. "Just like turning out the lights. And the King deserved a quick end. He's mighty old. Look at those teeth."

Hal was rough fleshing the skull. Several of the molars had been ground down to the gum line. The enamel was paper thin on many others. One of the canines was partially broken off.

"Life was getting pretty tough for the King," Hal said, then stopped talking as his knife gritted against an object under the bear's tongue.

"It's a plague taked base and jacket of a bullet," Hal said. "Look at that."

The old, corroded .30 caliber bullet had been lodged in the muscle and gristle under the bear's tongue, facing upward toward the roof of the mouth.

"That bullet must have done two things to the King," Hal said when we returned to base camp. "It must have made him mighty distrustful of humans and given him a sore mouth for a long time. Wonder what happened to the guy that put it there?"

The bullet hadn't kept the bear from growing. Fleshed out he measured 7' 9" long and 8' 10¼" across the claw tips for a square of 8' 3 5/8". These same rough measurements put his skull at 10" wide and 15½" long for a total of 25½" which, even allowing for shrinkage and precision measurements, put him in tie position for 12th place in the Boone and Crockett Club's "Records of North American Big Game."

Kay and Bob shake hands over the fallen monarch.

Toward the end of the measuring and salting processes, Hal rose from his knees, cocked his head in a listening posture, cautiously sniffed the air and placed his finger before his lips for silence.

Bob, Dale and I looked around for our guns, somewhat mystified that Hal would start tip-toeing weaponless toward a possible quarry.

Still sniffing, he headed for the cook tent, cautiously peered through the closed flaps for a moment then tip-toed back to his work.

"I'll be plague taked if Kay hasn't remembered her promise and coaxed some blueberry pies from that Yukon stove."

That night we silently raised two forkfuls of the delicacy in tribute—one to Kay for her prowess as a baker and the other to the dethroned King of the Chetaslina.

And I'll be plague taked if it didn't seem the proper thing to do. ■

145

The Alaskan Grizzly

Hal and a prime grizzly.

By HAL WAUGH

Inevitably, whether sitting around a campfire in an unmapped part of the Kuskokwim, drinking coffee in an Arctic cabin or glassing a slope on Kodiak Island, my clients' discussions work around to the grizzly bear. After they've had their say, they'll ask, "what do you think, Hal?"

My answer is usually the same.

The words "grizzly bear" seem to excite the senses of sportsmen. Nice honest fellows who wouldn't cheat their neighbors, never sniped candy from the 5 & 10 as kids, and who drop their tithe in the collection plate on Sunday, are capable of concocting the wildest tales concerning grizzlies—and tell them so many times that apparently they believe their own fantastic stories. Experienced hunters and guides scoff at most of these tales, and rightfully so. But wait. One of the first and most important considerations to learn about the grizzly bear is: Some bear are entirely unpredictable. They do not follow a pattern of behavior. Biologists in the field may well become complacent, and capable guides gradually fall into the class of "familiarity breeds contempt," but if this attitude continues throughout a lifetime of experience, our rescue groups and search units may well have another bear mauling victim to work on.

Grizzly bear are not large when compared to some of the top trophies in the world, but a grizzly has many faculties and senses, and abilities that certainly place him well up in the top bracket of the world's most dangerous animals. He has a superior intelligence. Once wounded he seems immune to shock. He has courage beyond belief, and, surprisingly to some, he is one of the fastest and quickest of all animals.

My African experience is certainly limited, but 60 days of safari, gunning experience with two elephant, two rhino, one leopard, one lion, and considerable plains game, gives some basis of comparison between African and Alaskan game. In my opinion, our Alaskan grizzly is definitely one of the most capable and dangerous of all animals.

On two occasions I was deep in a herd of Cape buffalo. Not a comforting feeling, but a position I would certainly choose in preference to an equal size herd of Alaskan grizzly, were such a thing possible.

One experience with grizzly which stands out in my memory, happened a few years back while guiding a client from the central states. After a tiring climb through muskeg for a grizzly that I had spotted early in the day, we were suddenly confronted with a wildlife show, unstaged. Directly below us a cow moose and her calf burst out of a willow thicket and trotted swiftly across the muskeg. Alerted, I watched. Soon the grizzly that either spooked them or was actually hunting them, charged out of the willows in pursuit. At my word "shoot," the client fired and the grizzly whirled back into the willows. There was no way to tell if the bullet had connected.

Cautiously we worked down to the spot where the bear had been. All I could find was a little torn muskeg where the bear had swapped ends and gone back into the willows. I stationed the hunter down the hill where he had an unobstructed view of the area below us, and returned to the torn muskeg. It was a lonesome job going down through the willows trying to locate a possibly wounded grizzly. There was really only one route for me, an opening rather like a corridor angling down through the willows. After about 15 feet of tingling, slow progress I managed to catch a glimpse of movement, ever so slight, out of my left eye. It was the grizzly waiting for me, just above the corridor, in an ideal spot for an easy assassination of its tormentor. Only the flick of an ear gave it away. This was what I had seen. It required several moments of hard concentration on my part to make out the form of the well concealed bear. A neck shot at about 10 to 12 feet completed the story. My examination showed that the hunter's shot was too far back of the shoulders to prove instantly fatal, and yet not punishing enough to impair the bear's lethal actions and ability. Few animals would have the intelligence and courage, and vindictiveness, to set up the trap I could easily have blundered into.

Such an experience with a grizzly proves beyond doubt to the participants that here we have real danger, real excitement, and a highly valuable trophy when hanging on a wall at home or laying in front of the fireplace in the trophy room.

A word of caution when comparing the grizzly with the huge Alaska brown bear or the true Kodiak bear from Kodiak and Afognak Islands. Remember that a good big man can do everything a good little man can do, only better and in a more deadly way. Like big men, the larger bear are usually mild natured compared to grizzlies, but don't bet on it. Both bear have every attribute for the perfect animal fighting machine. ■

Blackies Are Smart

W. R. Weber

Wherever he is found, the blackie is a first class trophy.

151

By HAL WAUGH

Many experienced big game hunters fail to appreciate the worth of the black bear. Let them concentrate upon black bear hunting only, and I feel certain that their appreciation for these crafty and clever animals will increase. After a season or two they may be heard to remark, "Deer? Phooey. Caribou? Too simple. Moose? Big, and nice. Blackies? Let me tell you about the time . . . "

The black bear makes a beautiful trophy, whether it be a head mount or a full rug, and the average dwelling can accommodate a trophy of this size whereas the larger grizzlies and brownies are bulky and require more space.

Here in Alaska, most of the black bears taken during the hunting season are incidental to other hunting. The black bear may be seen above timber line, possibly on the mountaintop while one is hunting sheep or goats. He may be found in the valleys or on the muskegs while one hunts moose or caribou. Or the alert hunter may spot him in heavy timber. Wherever he is found, the blackie is a first class trophy.

Resident Alaskans who hunt black bears for meat kill them early in the spring, soon after the end of their dormant period, or late in the fall when their diet consists of berries. (Salmon-fed bear meat is not recommended.) Although mountain sheep flesh has long been considered the ultimate in palatable game meat, many a hunter, including myself, has said while gorging on tender bear steaks or chops, "This is as delicious as sheep!"

The black is the luckiest animal in the bush. He is also the smartest. He feeds and grazes at two or three miles an hour. His senses of smell and hearing are remarkable. Though near-sighted, his eyes are much better than commonly believed.

I agree with these generalities, and could add a few of my own.

Unfortunately, our Alaskan black bears have never been afforded the protection they deserve. Trigger-happy homesteaders, servicemen, construction workers, Sunday sportsmen and, worst of all, oldtimers who still believe the bugaboo tales told by their ancestors, are inclined to shoot any and every black bear they stumble across.

152

Females with baby cubs are not exempt from this slaughter. To make matters worse, most of these bears are killed during the summer months, when the flesh is useless and the pelts are impossible for trophies.

To hunt black bears, the first step is of course to go where they are known to be. Professional guides and experienced hunters may not agree upon the best course from here on, but a few facts hold true for all.

Good binoculars are more important than the make, caliber, sights and so forth of the rifle.

Patience is not only a virtue but a necessity, as the hunter may be required to spend hours trying to locate a shiny black object that is ducking under brush, hurrying here and there, swapping ends, and always alert.

We assume a bear is seen. He is high, and we'll have to make a fast trip to get into shooting position. This, however, is the bear's lucky day. Puffing and panting from our exertion, we reach what we hoped would be our vantage point and see him climbing straight up the mountain, away from us. The wind has not changed, and the muskeg afforded us soft, quiet going. But there he is, leaving the country.

Another time, luck may be in favor of the hunter and the bear comes easy.

Several years ago I managed to guide a Midwestern client to three blackies in two days. One of the three really came easy. I had watched him bed down on a slight rise in the terrain, and it was a simple matter to take the hunter up where he had a 20-foot shot. The bear was sleeping so soundly we could hear his snoring for the last 80 feet of our approach.

Could be that this hunter tells his Midwestern cronies how easy it is to bag a black bear. The next time he may have to hunt until he is exhausted, and then find he is fortunate to have one bear in a week.

The selection of rifles and calibers is too wide and varied for the isolation of a "best" bear gun. The average deer rifle should be satisfactory. The all-important issue for the hunter is, know the rifle and its capabilities in your hands.

Next in importance is the selection of a proper bullet, as everything available over the counter is not necessarily good. A nondisintegrating bullet of the Core-Lokt, Nosler or new Silver-Tip type should be used. At times the black bear can absorb a terrific amount of shock and punishment. A gut-shot black, though knocked off his feet, may bounce up like a rubber ball and run a mile and a half to die a slow, horrible death deep in the brush—inhumane, and the loss of a fine game animal.

I find my enthusiasm for rifle practice and the game of judging distance a difficult proposition to put over to some of my clients. A

Hal "turns" an ear on a blackie pelt.

few actually feel that, with all the progress of modern technology, surely a big arms manufacturing concern can install sights and "shoot in" a rifle at the factory more efficiently than the hunter himself can do it. This is so absurd that it deserves little comment.

Others feel they are too busy—just can't take time off from business to practice with a hunting rifle. Then there are those who "had Jim Doakes sight 'er in down on the police range. She's shootin' dead center at fifty feet."

Well! All you can do is explain patiently that each individual must sight in his own firearm to suit his individual requirements.

The other extreme, pleasant for the guide, are the hunters and riflemen who know the trajectory of their ammunition and guns, and use it.

One of my repeat hunters is a joy to guide. He shoots twelve months of the year, and makes an avocation of hand loading. He understands exactly what his bullet will do, and what his rifle can do. This man is one of the world's outstanding scientists, but if he didn't practice continually, we could not enjoy so many one-shot kills from my camps during his hunts.

The sighting equipment for bear hunting can vary according to the terrain and the hunter's personal choice or need. Many men require a telescope sight as an optical aid. Others find the receiver sights completely satisfactory. A very limited number still cling to the old rear sight standard on many guns.

My choice for an all-around rifle is a Griffin & Howe double lever side mount and the Lyman 48 receiver sight.

On foggy or rainy days the 'scope is left in camp. When the weather is satisfactory and the day doesn't promise a lot of brush crawling, the 'scope can be used.

Black bear hunting has much to recommend it. It can take the sportsman into the wild beauty of the mountaintops, spoken of in awe by sheep and goat hunters. It can be a true test of his hunting ability, marksmanship and stamina. The epicure can relish the meat, if it is given anything like the care lavished on prime beef.

Best of all, for the trophy hunter, when the little woman gets busy with her housecleaning, this scamp of the woods stands a better chance of staying than do more ponderous trophies. ∎

Blackie Wouldn't Say "No"

A prime blackie makes a good rug.

By CHARLES J. KEIM

Until Blackie arrived the hunt had been thoroughly enjoyable, although all the moose that we had seen within shooting distance near the lake in the Alaska Range of mountains were cows and calves.

Dr. Neil W. Hosley and I had been flown by bush plane into the remote area to try to get our winter's meat supply before the fall instruction would begin at the University of Alaska where Neil was the dean at that time.

We watched great numbers of ducks and geese noisily set down for food and rest before they continued their flights southward from a land that Jack Frost already had tinged with a medley of colors. Muskrats and beaver worked in the lake and disappeared momentarily

157

when a swan settled down to add its white beauty to the placid surface. Several loons lent their lonely, haunting cries to the scene as though mourning the fact that an unfeeling Old Man Winter soon would grip the land in his icy hand.

Our bush pilot was scheduled to pick us up the next day and, although gameless, we were almost content that late afternoon to simply drink in all the beauty of an undisturbed nature.

Then Blackie entered the scene, stole the show, and forced us reluctantly to lower the curtain on him.

I left Neil for a short while to determine if a lake nearby was large enough to accommodate the float plane.

"We had a visitor while you were gone, Chuck," Neil said upon my return. "He was a black bear. I was glassing the lake when he walked down that game trail, saw me, then laid down in the grass and peered at me from about 15 yards away. I hollered at him and even banged an empty gasoline can against a tree to scare him. But he wouldn't scare. Finally I threw a stick at him and he got up with a real injured air and walked down to feed on that old moose offal left by the previous party. Then he looked back at me like I was being inhospitable, and walked away."

The blackies I have hunted in Montana, Washington State and Alaska always have spooked like deer at the smallest noise, and I told Neil so. He agreed that his previous experiences with blackies had pretty well paralleled mine, although they are unpredictable at times.

We watched the lake for a while, then Blackie walked down the same game trail to pay us both a visit, and he was mighty unpredictable.

I shouted "hello" to him and he put on all four brakes and sat down about 15 yards away and looked at us. I picked up my camera and .30-'06, hoping to get a picture of our visitor who was plump and sported a glistening black coat. He smiled once then suddenly got shy before I could focus my camera. Then he walked off the trail and laid down and peered through a few sparse grass blades at us. His muzzle was hidden and he evidently thought that the remainder of his approximately 250 pounds was camouflaged by those little grass blades.

158

I shouted and he didn't budge. Both Neil and I then sat down and watched him. He watched back. After 10 minutes of this watching game, Blackie gave up and headed toward moose offal where he fed while I watched him with my binoculars and Neil glassed him with his rifle scope.

We then directed our attention back to the lake, thinking that Blackie would feed and disappear.

But not that black clown. He fed for a time then walked right toward us. We didn't want to turn our backs on him and didn't want to shoot such a friendly fellow. Besides the blackie season wouldn't open for two days.

What does one do when a black bear starts sidling toward one with all the friendly spirit of a St. Bernard dog, and a lot bigger?

We did the obvious. We took some pictures, then stepped aside. Blackie again headed in our direction. We both rather vehemently told him that he was unwelcome. Besides, he was so close that we could tell that he had halitosis from his meal.

But Blackie wouldn't take no. He kept right on walking, then stumbled onto the old moose head left by the earlier party.

Blackie grabbed that head, antlers and all, like a hungry dog seizes a bone. He picked it up in his mouth and started to stumble away with it. Twice his front legs tangled in the antlers and he plowed to a stop. Then he stumbled away again—only this last time he headed toward our tent.

Like two angry traffic policemen, we shouted at him to change direction. Like a deaf motorist, he kept right on going. He stumbled through some thick brush and we hurried around it, certain that by the time we reached our tent Blackie would have it torn to shreds because our grub was inside, behind the zippered mosquito netting.

When we reached the tent we saw Blackie rubbing himself with some plastic sheeting like a cat with catnip. I had brought the material to protect meat from possible rain, and had left it outside the tent. Blackie had dropped the moose head approximately 20 feet from the plastic and had made a beeline for the stuff. He rubbed one side of his head with the plastic, then rubbed the other. He lovingly and slobberingly caressed it—totally oblivious of our presence. Finally he rolled on it, right at the tent entrance.

"I'm going to have to bust him, Chuck," Neil said. "I don't want him to tear up the tent after he spots the grub."

"Maybe I can scare him with my rifle," I said.

I fired the bullet right over his head.

Blackie didn't even wince.

He spotted the grub, dropped the plastic like he had dropped the moose head, and scooped out the front of the tent with one slash of his right paw.

Neil's .30-'06 roared. Blackie crumpled, his nose just inside the tent.

We skinned out Blackie and wrapped his hams in sheeting. The next day the bush pilot flew us all out. The meat went to a charitable institution; the hide went to the U. S. Fish and Wildlife Service and we went home a little sad and puzzled about Blackie who wouldn't take "no."

In the years that followed many varied experiences with the black bear strengthened my views about their unpredictability. One experience that made me hope that I could predict what a black bear would do occurred when I was camped along Indian River in Interior Alaska with my wife, Betty, and our daughter, Ann, 8, and son Bruce, 6.

When a noise near our tent awakened me at 4:10 a.m., I cautiously awakened the family, then peered outside. Sure enough, a large black bear was sniffing around our food, located approximately 30 feet away.

I shouted, then fired my Smith and Wesson .44 magnum revolver over the animal's head. It fell over itself in its eagerness to get out of camp.

At 4:40 a.m. I again awoke when I heard another sound. Through the translucent nylon tent I could see and hear a black bear sniffing the length of my son who was sleeping next to one of the tent walls. That bear should not have returned so soon.

I did not have much time to ponder this new problem. Certainly I should not attempt to awaken my family and in so doing perhaps startle the bear into viciousness. Sitting up in my sleeping bag, I pointed my revolver at the bear's muzzle as it began to enter the tent flap. I did not want to shoot, nor did I want to risk the trauma of a confined explosion awakening my family while a bloody black bear was threshing around at the entrance of our shelter.

"If I hit the bear before its eye enters the tent, perhaps the blow will push the nose out of the tent and the startled animal will run away," I hastily thought—and hoped.

Still holding the revolver in my right hand, I hit the bear on the nose as hard as I could with my left fist.

"Get out of here!" I shouted. The family sat upright in their sleeping bags and Blackie ran.

Calming down my family, I carefully peered out the tent. Approximately 30 yards away was a black bear sitting on its haunches and looking aggrievedly at the big green thing that had hit it.

It was a smaller, different bear. This one reluctantly departed only after I fired three shots over its head.

We returned to Fairbanks that afternoon as we had planned, certain that had we stayed we would have had real trouble with our unpredictable and uninvited guests. ■

Mixed Bag
From The Kuskokwim

Jerry, with rifle, and Larry look over the blonde grizzly.

By CHARLES J. KEIM

"Try to sit down; he's probably just curious and will walk away," I told Phyllis Scheuerman. "Don't make any fast motions. He might spook the larger ones. The wind is blowing in our direction. That's one point in our favor."

"About the only one, it seems." Phil grinned, her white, even teeth contrasting sharply with the tan she had accumulated the past few days while climbing peaks after Dall or white sheep in an as yet unmapped portion of the Kuskokwim country in the westerly part of central Alaska.

Neither of us really could sit. My pack, loaded with rope, spotting 'scope, ammunition, hatchet and all the other gear a registered guide needs, would have prevented me from doing so even if I'd been inclined to risk lacerating my rump on the sharp porphyritic rock that clung to the approximately 65-degree slope of the toughest peak we'd yet encountered. And Phil was standing next to a deep slide of the stuff that would necessitate some fast, boot tearing footwork before we'd get across.

Phil crouched as best she could. She still faced the half-curl ram that was approximately 100 yards above us. He suddenly had stepped into one of the many saddles that ran like the wavy edge of a bread knife blade to the uppermost peaks where we'd spotted several big sheep from the creek bed, now so far below us that it resembled a spider web on a green lawn.

"What's he doing now?" I asked, not daring to risk turning around.

"Darn thing has laid down and he's still looking right at us," Phil answered.

Resignedly, I carefully wedged one boot heel against what I hoped was a more securely anchored rock and again scanned the wild country below and in the distance.

A late August 1961 snow already had re-silvered the peaks. The frost-touched vegetation on the lower slopes of the mountain behind us looked like a multi-colored Persian rug. At any other time I'd have enjoyed this ever changing view, but now the rock I was bracing against began to uproot, starting a small slide of rocks that tumbled metallically down the slope. I half stood, then nodded to Phil who gratefully straightened up for a moment.

"Let's move away from him and stay at this level," I said, twisting my body and hazarding a quick look upward at the ram.

We moved rapidly through the loose rock, then slowed down for a moment while I stripped the leaves from a solitary alpine plant and tossed them up to check the wind. Then we scrambled down and over a small ravine. I took a last look at the ram before we moved from his view. He still was lying down and looking right at us.

We rested for a few moments, then carefully worked upward through a jumble of boulders, slides and high stacks of flat shale slabs that threatened to topple at any moment. I was beginning to get apprehensive about the wind because the higher we climbed the more apt we were to encounter vagrant, swirling currents that could carry our scent to the big ones we were after. I wasn't worried about the occasional rocks we dislodged. Sheep, like goats, live with these.

Phil gamely stayed up with me. I'd let her set the pace the first two days of the hunt so I had a pretty good idea about how far we could go before we should take a breather. I signalled for her to follow closely as I skirted around another half-curl ram that was standing on a ledge approximately 25 yards below us. We could have dropped a rock on him he was so oblivious of our presence.

Soon there was only one way to go, and that was almost straight up a narrow sheep trail approximately 14 inches wide with massive, house-size boulders to our right and hundreds of feet of emptiness to our left. Our rifles were slung over our shoulders and we were using our gloved hands to help work upward.

Suddenly through a notch between two boulders I saw three sheep. I ground squirrel whistled to Phil to hold up for a moment, and pointed. Then grasping a ledge above me, I looked back to see if she had heard and understood. I lifted one hand and extended three fingers and pointed to our right. Phil nodded then signalled with one finger. I nodded negatively and again held up three fingers. She grinned, nodded that she understood, then pointed straight ahead of me and again held up one finger.

I looked up. Blocking our trail was a half-curl ram, no more than 30 yards ahead. I vainly tried to press more closely against the rock to hide from his steady, inquisitive gaze.

He stood there and we stood there and he had the advantage because he didn't have to hold onto rocks to keep from tumbling into the chasm far below. The three sheep I'd spotted disappeared while we clung there. They were two ewes and a lamb.

"Get the hell out of our way," I muttered at the half-curl, then mentally added a "please," because if he'd take off suddenly he might spook the others that surely were above us, and he only could go up.

I heard Phil suppressing a laugh.

"Well, if this is going to turn into an endurance contest, he has all the advantages," I said to Phil. "Maybe if we talk a little he'll take off."

So we talked, wondering if our luck now would run like that of several days earlier when a caribou had followed Phil, her husband, Gerald or "Jerry," and his guide, indefatigable Larry Keeler, and me for several miles despite our efforts to spook him away, then, when we were climbing after three rams had trotted far ahead of us, climbed right between the sheep and scattered them before we had even begun the final sneak.

The half-curl listened imperturbably to our conversation, and for a time I actually was afraid that he would lie down.

"Well, I'm getting tired holding onto these rocks," I said at length. I grasped a loose rock and pounded it against the cliffside. The ram looked at us more intently then walked from view.

"Let's go," I said.

Phil sighed as she changed her cramped position. We climbed a few steps upward, then the ram reappeared. Again I clanked rock against rock and when the ram refused to budge I threw the rock up at him. The missile fell short because I had little free throwing room. I threw several more rocks and he finally started trotting up the trail.

"The rest of the hunting party will never believe this," Phil commented, and I agreed, but we'd sure tell them. There had been a bit of friendly banter about which party would have the most fun and get the best trophies, and Phil, Jerry, Larry and I had done our share of enthusiastic talking.

Phil and her trophy Kuskokwim Dall ram.

Actually, Hal Waugh, guide and outfitter, was operating quite an Alaskan "safari" that fall. Now they were in the spike camps. Frederick Boyle, director of athletics at the University of Alaska, was guiding Charles Erwin Wilson, Jr.; Clark Engle was guiding Leo Renault, Jr.; and Hank Marshall was guiding Howard H. Fitzgerald. Erwin, the son of the late U.S. Secretary of Defense and president of General Motors, operates The Sportsman in Birmingham, Michigan, and Leo is a business associate. Howard is a business manager and vice president of *The Pontiac Press*. All three are close friends and the kind of outdoorsmen a guide likes to meet. Helping out as packers were my nephew, Frank Keim, Jr., who had hitchhiked to Alaska from Ontario to attend the University of Alaska, Joel Rudinger, graduate student in English at the University, and Richard Palmiter, a student from Poughkeepsie. When Hal's wife, Julie, had flown out from base camp before the hunt, their 14-year-old son, Dan, had remained to help out generally, and he later succeeded in getting a Dall.

Undoubtedly we'd all have yarns to swap when we'd return to base camp. I'd never thrown rocks at Dall sheep before and I wondered how many of my associates at the University of Alaska would believe me—probably as many as would the friends of Phil and Jerry back in Minneapolis where he is an insurance company executive.

"Well, we'll have to get a sheep for some kind of proof," I told Phil. By now we were on the steep ridge leading to the top peak which was crowned by a large rock approximately six feet square. The ridge Y'd out there and apparently sloped downward.

"I'm going to crawl up to that rock," I told Phil. "If the rams we saw from the creek are still around they're to the right or left and below us. I'll give you the high sign when I take a look."

As I crawled to the rock, I looked for the sheep we'd evidently driven ahead of us, but he was out of sight. When I reached the rock I threw some of my pipe tobacco into the air to check the wind. It was blowing from our right so the best chances were that there would be sheep to our right. I wriggled out of my pack and carefully looked down the ridge from the base of the rock.

There was a sheep, a ram, a big one approximately 250 yards below. I carefully looked him over with my binoculars. I could see one of his horns, more than full curl, and damned if he wasn't asleep in a slight depression with a steep drop to his left and right. Then three, more than full curl rams appeared from around a rock. I slid backwards a few feet and signalled to Phil. We crawled behind the rock and mounted the spotting 'scope. The 30-power lens told us that any one of the sheep would make a fine trophy. One of the three had horns with more flare than the others, but the sleeper had massive horns ending with slightly broomed tips.

"Take your choice," I said to Phil, admittedly feeling like a jeweler holding our four diamonds to a customer.

She decided on the sleeper, whispering meanwhile what I was thinking—"How I wish that Jerry were here, too." Both of the Scheuermans had shot bighorns in British Columbia and other game elsewhere, so Phil knew what to do with the .308. She pulled her sight far enough back on the big fellow so she'd not risk breaking a horn or damaging the cape, then squeezed the trigger.

As the shot crashed above the sound of the now brisk breeze and echoed back and forth with diminishing strength, the ram half rose to a sitting position then began to slump downward.

"Do it again," I said to Phil, remembering a ram I'd taken earlier that seemingly had dropped at the first shot then after a wait had run crazily, and then bloodily had rolled far down the mountain slope.

The remaining three rams jumped again at the second shot, but stamped uncertainly about the dead ram.

"He's their leader, and they're confused. Maybe they think he's still sleeping and unworried," I said to Phil. She nodded in agreement.

I rolled a cigarette, hoping that the other rams would take off, but not spook out and travel so far that Jerry and Larry wouldn't want to try for them next day.

The rams still were there when I finished the smoke.

"Well, it's getting late and I still have a sheep to skin out," I said, so we slowly began walking toward the rams. They looked apprehensively at us then at the fallen animal. Their courage broke when we were approximately 30 feet from them, and they bounded away from us, the ram with the flared horns leading. In a few seconds they were out of sight.

As I dressed and caped out the ram we heard a sharp whistle far below us. On another ridge and separated from us by a tremendous canyon were Jerry and Larry. They'd seen the sheep from spike camp and had decided to go after them. Now they indicated by sign language that they planned to take after the remaining three rams.

As we worked, my nephew, Frank, made the climb up the long ridge from spike camp. He'd watched the action from spike camp after he'd returned from base camp where Hal had provided him with fresh supplies.

That night we ascertained that Phil's ram probably would just make "the book," then watched a flashlight bobbing up and down as Jerry and Larry made their way back to camp bearing the ram with the flared horns. Jerry had taken the now spooky animal with a fantastic 650-yard shot with his scoped .308.

We were a pretty elated hunting party as we sat around the campfire that night–happy because we now could concentrate on getting a grizzly or two which Jerry and Phil wanted to mount full size for their new home.

"I couldn't see you and Phil, but I could see the sheep," Frank said as we ate delicious Dall liver. "I was wondering who had taken the ram when I first saw you walking toward them. I had a ringside seat with my binoculars, almost as good as when we watched you getting your caribou, Jerry."

That started us talking about the magnificent double-shovel caribou now back in base camp that Jerry had gotten several days earlier when we'd been hunting another drainage.

All five of us had been together that day, walking down the wide bed of the greatly braided Post River and on the lookout for sheep, caribou or moose. Phil had the moose tag, Jerry the caribou tag, and both had one for a grizzly. Grizzly season still wouldn't open until September 1.

We'd seen a number of ewes and lambs, and several smaller caribou and were considering heading back to spike camp when I again decided to glass the slopes we'd walked past. I'd learned long ago that the hunter covers only one-half the country when he just looks ahead.

Through my binoculars I saw a flash of white on a small hill that sloped from a large peak like a massive buttress on a building. A caribou was feeding there, but I wanted to take a closer look before I called the attention of my hunting companions. Obligingly, the animal fed his way up to the crown of the hill then looked over the countryside for a few moments.

"Holy Cow," I blurted out, then hastily dug for the spotting 'scope.

I focussed on the animal while he still stood there, then hastily beckoned to Larry then Jerry to take a look.

Even from approximately 2,000 yards away we could make out the large beam, wide top palms and at least one shovel.

The animal would require a stalk almost like that for a sheep. And there was some question if he'd remain on the hill. He settled that for us by feeding down the slope once more then lying down.

Since Jerry had the caribou tag and Larry was his guide, I somewhat enviously watched them take off.

"Might as well sit down and watch this," I said. I placed the 'scope in a more advantageous position, put on the 20-power eyepiece to provide a wider field of view for Phil, then suggested that Frank and I sit down against a driftwood log and watch with our 7x35 binoculars. I was pretty hopeful. If the caribou should get up, he'd probably continue to feed on the side of the hill because he was in a small meadow almost surrounded by large rocks. Of course there was always the possibility that he'd pick his way through the rocks or climb back up and disappear from sight.

Both Jerry and Larry were in top physical condition and good hunters. I wasn't worried about mistakes.

The two men disappeared for a time into a fringe of spruce that straggled part way up the hill. While they were out of sight we began munching our sandwiches.

Both Jerry and Phil had told us at the onset that they weren't particularly interested in getting animals that would go in "the book," but I couldn't help telling Phil that I thought that the caribou would go at least 50th in the volume. He was big!

"Don't you dare tell Jerry that until we measure the animal—if we get him," Phil said.

"If we get him," I agreed, and we again watched the stalk.

The caribou got up after a time and again commenced feeding. We watched the two men head to the right of the hill as they broke from

171

the cover of the trees, then crouch and half crawl around the protective slope to keep out of the wind and sight of the bull.

When they were about 100 yards from the caribou, the animal began feeding away from them, and they hastened their climb up the hillside, cutting toward him.

"Something's got to happen soon; they're almost in sight of the bull," I commented. I heard Phil breathe, "Get him, Jerry."

The bull bent down to crop another mouthful of lichens. Suddenly all three of us saw him fall heavily to his side. Then we heard the craaaack! of a rifle. We watched the two men close the approximately 70-yard gap between themselves and the caribou. Jerry did a short dance, signalled victory to his fans in the river bed, and began taking pictures.

When we reached the hill, the caribou was almost skinned out. Careful, conservative measurements back in base camp a couple of days later put the total score at 424 plus, a tie for 21st place in the 1958 book.

We had debated at the start of the hunt whether or not we should hunt together or split up into two parties each day as we'd leave spike camp. So far, our decision to hunt occasionally as a group had paid off in trophies.

This same fact held true as we started out for grizzly. We had seen a number of these animals while we were after caribou and sheep, but the season hadn't been open. The next one we saw wasn't a bit interested in hanging around to give us a shot, and he displayed an exhibition of stamina which boosted my already high opinion and respect for these animals.

We were angling along a mountainside when we saw him doing the same on the other. A creek separated us and we were approximately 600 yards apart. Some contrary breeze gave him our scent before we could even put our glasses on him to judge for size and condition of coat. He lifted his head, sniffed, then ran along the mountainside. He stopped for an instant, then changed directions and began running straight up the mountain. He headed for the highest peak and stopped but twice to breathe heavily before continuing his run which took him from our sight in approximately 12 minutes.

We were disappointed, of course, but there was more to come after that exciting exhibition. We were approximately two-thirds of the way back to spike camp when Larry, who was leading, stopped, carefully focussed his binoculars and confounded us all with the startling exclamation: "Good Lord, Chuck, I've got me a polar bear!"

We all looked at the flat meadow near a mountain base far down the canyon we were skirting. Even without our binoculars we could see a large, almost white object slowly meandering around from berry patch to berry patch. I set up the 'scope then whistled as I beckoned to my companions. The animal was a medium size, almost white grizzly bear which aptly fitted Jerry's statement that it resembled "a giant panda bear." I'd seen only one other like it in my travels about Alaska and it had been taken by Robert Rausch, now game management supervisor for Interior and Arctic Alaska for the Alaska Department of Fish and Game. Bob later agreed that they are relatively rare when he agreed with my contention that few women take the Dall sheep in Alaska as had Phil.

We hastily agreed that Jerry and Larry should go after the blonde grizzly, and they were on their way before Phil and I again had settled back in a ringside seat for one of the most exciting bear stalks I'd yet seen.

For a long 25 minutes we alternately watched Jerry and Larry scrambling down the mountain, and the bear unconcernedly feeding. Then as the hunters reached the bottom of the canyon and began crossing the creek and moving out of our sight for a time, the bear suddenly reared up on its hind legs, its mahogany colored front paws dangling from its chest like those of a giant ground squirrel. Then the bear whirled and raced toward a small canyon and disappeared from sight.

"He's gone," Phil and I groaned in unison, then looked for Jerry and Larry. They had scrambled up the high creek bank and were carefully stalking toward the wedge of neck high bushes that would screen them from where they last had seen the bear.

"What a disappointment . . . ," I began to say, when suddenly the bear reappeared from the small canyon and started loping back to the berry bushes where it had been feeding before it had made its hasty flight.

"Get ready, Jerry, oh, get ready," Phil breathed. Then, "Good Lord, they're going to bump into each other!"

Scarcely daring to breathe myself, I watched the bear and the two men walking toward the point of bushes that screened the hunters from their quarry. Then I watched them simultaneously walk around the point and close the distance separating them to about 60 yards.

For what seemed like long minutes, but in reality couldn't have been more than 20 seconds, we watched the bear again rear up while Jerry held up his rifle and Larry focussed his glasses on the bear to determine condition of pelt. Jerry and Larry later told me that the latter's only comment was, understandably, "I'm having a hard time focussing these glasses. Take it!"

We watched the bear drop to all fours and start running. Then it lurched and whirled as the sound of a shot, followed by others, echoed up the mountain.

The sow had dropped in the creek bed, and we skinned her out for a full body mount while Jerry and Phil held the flashlights. Jerry said that he planned to have the taxidermist give her the same inquisitive stance Phil and I had witnessed during the stalk.

We were quite certain that our party had fared as well as the rest. When we returned to base camp, Hal confirmed our belief. Total bag for the party was six sheep, with Phil's the largest; four grizzlies; five caribou, and one moose. We could have made that two moose, for after Phil and I had made an exciting 75-minute stalk through three bulls to reach the big one up front, she declined to take him after looking him over from approximately 60 yards.

But she and Jerry were content. The trophy room in their new home in Minneapolis would have some permanent reminders of a good mixed bag hunt in Alaska's unmapped Kuskokwim. ■

North America's Premier Mountaineer

Dr. Robert Broadbent with a Wrangell Mountain goat.

Story and photos by HAL WAUGH
Reprinted from Alaska Sportsman® , June, 1962 (ALASKA® magazine)

It had taken a long time to reach the crest in these Kenai mountains. My hunting companion and I were doubtful and not just a little pessimistic concerning our chances for success. We were after mountain goat, those rugged beautiful animals of the heights. For days we had remained down in the valley confining our activities to fishing in the beaver ponds for golden fins and waiting for the rain to lessen. Today had seemed promising, but the higher we climbed, the lower ebbed our spirits, and not from rain . . . it was fog—the bane of goat hunters.

We had chosen a long hogback for our ascent and were plodding along with clouds of fog shifting about us, enveloping our world periodically in a billowing whiteness. I was somewhat ahead of Red Chaffin, who in everyday life functions as Station Manager for the Federal Aviation Administration at Kodiak. Red, my friend and hunting companion for many years, was finding goat hunting more arduous after eleven months at a desk. Then suddenly through a breach in the vapors I detected two goats working in our direction from a higher level. What luck! We could sit down and wait until they walked within easy shooting range.

After waiting a considerable length of time for Red to catch up with me, I started back down the hogback, feeling that he must have spotted something that I had failed to see. Red came into view a long way down the mountain, walking directly away from me. Wonderingly and somewhat uneasy I hurried after him. When I knew that I was within his hearing, I signaled by whistling. Red stopped, swung about, threw up his arms in a gesture of resignation and despair, and began retracing his weary steps up the steep incline. Mine had not been the first whistle he heard. He had been betrayed and led astray by a "whistler," a whistling marmot which is plentiful in this goat country. Red thought I had changed my direction. Together we again climbed the ridge, pausing frequently to wait out the haziness.

One of the most impressive memories of a long hunting career was the sight that greeted us during one of our waiting periods. The fog began to dissipate. Visibility became better and we found that we were seated above a small amphitheater nestled high in the crags. The sun was seeping through a misty prism, offering a fantastically artistic scene. As if in further reward for our climb, two goats slowly entered the setting. They were faintly discernible at first; each step absorbed them more definitely into the panorama. Nature's lofty beauty was being indelibly etched in our memories.

178

Goats and blackies are often found feeding within sight of each other in places like these Kenai ridges where Clyde Fogg scored on both species.

The stillness of the atmosphere was in our favor. Another 200 yards of wandering would put our trophies in reasonable shooting range if some vagrant breeze did not carry our scent upward to interfere with their confident, unsuspecting stroll. Goat stews and tasty breakfast chops were not far off at this point. After all, we were as interested in the additional meat supply as in the shaggy, thick white wolly hides and jet black rapier-like horns. The mountaintop drama unfolded according to the script. Red took his cue and I mine and each downed his selected one. Our '06's put our game down to stay. Then the work started. We slowly and painstakingly dressed each animal to give the meat the best possible care. The trip off the mountain was to prove a nightmare of effort. A foolish decision of the morning had started us up the mountain with only one packboard. With two goats to pack out we were in a predicament. As I was somewhat more used to packing, I made a carry out of my goat by tying the rear feet to the front feet and used the forelegs as pack straps. By lashing the head down securely, a pack of this type will suffice, all the while providing pure misery. We followed one of the many bear trails in our descent and never did a good trail seem more welcome than the one leading along the canyon down the valley to camp!

It is difficult for some of us who have lived on goat meat to understand the prejudice against this tasty and delicious game meat. One must assume the aversion stems from some mental association with the common farmyard goat. A simple study in the public library will quickly prove the mountain goat is not even remotely related to any of the domestic strains. It is a type of antelope, closer to the chamois and the serrow. The zoologist includes it in the ox family. Its food consists of mosses, lichens, buds and twigs. Mountain goat meat is prized by the Alaskan sportsman who lives in and around goat hunting country.

Goat hunting is far more dangerous than hunting the grizzly bear and the great brown. This fact is not due to any aggressiveness from the goat, but rather to the terrain the hunter must traverse while negotiating the animal's habitat. Comparatively few hunters have the will, the stamina, and the knowhow to ascend the jagged peaks after mountain goat. A few years ago two men lost their lives within 12 months and within a few airline miles of each other. One was an inexperienced young man, seriously in need of an experienced hunting companion or guide. He was a resident Alaskan, but a short time one. This young man could be living today had he known or been advised on the specific techniques and equipment goat hunting demands. He would not have worn leather soled shoes which caused him to slip and fall approximately 1,000 feet.

The second hunter was much older and more experienced, yet he fell from a trail and plunged down the mountainside to his death. Faulty equipment and lack of necessary precautions exact a grim price from the uninitiated, the careless, the incompetent.

Even with experience and well chosen equipment, goat hunting still can be dangerous due to the unknown, to nature's elements.

Jack Seidensticker, my Montana client, was all any guide could ask for. Jack was an experienced hunter, a gentleman in every respect, and a first rate companion. We had hunted sheep and moose in the Brooks Range, north of the Arctic Circle and now were hunting goat and black bear on the Kenai Peninsula. For days I had observed a fine big goat feeding and apparently living near a high mountain meadow above our camp. A vast expanse of glacier on one side of the meadow presented difficulties. However, we planned a strategy that would take us within shooting range. After gaining considerable altitude downwind from the goat, we began a parallel course to our quarry around the mountain. When we needed to take a breather, we stopped in a shoot or water course where the spring thaws had washed out a reasonably smooth area suitable for resting weary legs. Seating ourselves comfortably, our rifles and my pack stowed carefully nearby, we began to glass the opposite walls of the valley. Our relaxing moments were brief. A tumultuous, rumbling roar got us on our feet in an instant. Momentarily we could not determine the source and direction of the violence. Indecision ended abruptly as rocks the size of wash tubs came bounding by our resting spot. A frantic scramble back to the cliff we had just left offered the only available protection, doubtful as the six-inch overhang was. We'd need a lot of luck to go with it, considering Jack's 220 and my 190 pounds.

I assume the same thoughts, regrets, and fears flashed through our minds that all doomed men must have. Those were lonesome, poignant, agonizing moments that passed before the slide diminished and finally ceased altogether. We could glance over our shoulders from where we were pressed flat against the cliff and see hundreds of large boulders and rocks catapulting downward, exploding, with powdered rock and debris fanning upward and sideward. Any one of them could quickly have changed us into goat-hunter burgers, but the only one that touched us whipped by Jack's leg with a faint tug at his trousers. How the slide ever missed us, our rifles, and my pack was an awesome wonder. The only way we could have avoided this slide would have been to have gone after goat some other day. It was definitely "off season" for slides at this time of the year. Yet it happened.

We continued our careful stalk. A short time later we located our quarry just about where we had planned for him to be. He was feeding, unaware of our presence. The actual kill was devoid of excitement. We had had that already in our near brush with calamity.

The mounted head will require little space, but will be as handsome as any trophy and a reminder of a most thrilling hunt.

In prone position on a rocky knoll, we admired the shaggy whiskered magnificence of the great animal before us. When Jack felt calm and unruffled he aligned the bead of his old 30S Remington for a vital shot and squeezed the familiar trigger. The goat walked forward a few feet and collapsed. A one shot kill on goat is no mean feat, as they seem immune to shock.

Jack knew his rifle. He knew where it was shooting, where his 180 grain bullets would land. I place a higher value on a rifle proven by usage, rather than being a follower of the group who continually change guns and calibers, holding hotly contested arguments as to the comparative values of the calibers. Bullet choice proves more valuable than caliber in actual field work.

In collapsing, Jack's goat tumbled over the ledge which we figured would restrain him, and continued down the incline farther than we wanted him to. What condition would his horns be in when we got to him? We found the old gentleman well shaken up, but his sharp-pointed headgear was unscathed. Now Jack could head for Montana with his fine trophies and I could proceed with my next hunting parties.

Clyde Fogg had come from Michigan for goat and black bear. The amphibious plane had landed us on a high mountain lake. It was some distance to where we had planned to hunt so the last part of our trip must be with the faithful packboards strapped to our backs, carrying our entire camp. About halfway between the lake and our proposed hunting area, we spotted a goat high on the mountain. Pausing, we focused him in our binoculars. We could not judge goat trophy from this distance with any great degree of accuracy, but I told Clyde the body looked good to me. If we started the climb for it now we could expect to be caught by darkness high in the rugged Kenai mountains. We would endure the doubtful pleasure of siwashing it out during the hours of darkness in some accessible cave—if we could find one. Clyde had come from Michigan to Alaska for a goat, so we decided to gamble and go after this one.

We'd need to travel light, so we cached everything, except our rifles, and commenced our stiff climb.

The goat had bedded down, giving us the time we'd need to approach within shooting range. A high climb such as we were making takes much time. We had gained considerable altitude before he again was up and feeding towards the top of the mountain. The last critical period, the approach to reasonable shooting range, now required both speed and caution if we were to give Clyde a shot at this goat. I looked back over my shoulder to encourage my hunter to come along somewhat faster, and I was surprised to see him motionless pressed flat against the steep mountainside. My beckonings did not attract his attention. Instantly I began my descent, to Clyde's position. He was "frozen" fast to the mountain. After a little encouragement and reassurance, Clyde began climbing once more. I had to agree that this straight up and down country was a contrast to the flat Michigan country.

The last few yards before the shot were the kind the hunter likes to live over and over again. Thoughts were alternately filled with thrills and excitements, fears and apprehensions. We managed to keep rocks between us and the goat until Clyde had a good unobstructed shot at about 90 yards. Only one shot was required. The goat slipped and slid down the mountain, falling but a short distance, then coming to rest on a perfect place for skinning and dressing. I hurried down after Clyde's trophy to make sure he didn't revive and wobble away to be lost forever. This precaution was unnecessary.

Time was the all-important factor now if we were to reach our camping location by dark. Knowing Clyde would want photographs of his first goat trophy, I would have to delay the dressing and skinning. But where was Clyde? After waiting a few impatient minutes, I started back up the mountain to see what had happened to detain my hunter. Not far from the location of the shooting, there was Clyde, again frozen flat the mountain. I joined him on the cliffside and in a short time we were on the move again. In the days following, we had many laughs over it and the movement Clyde developed which permitted him to descend quite rapidly. He utilized a simple, froglike movement sitting down, extending his heels and sliding on the seat of his pants until he reached his heels again. Unfortunately, I had no movie camera to record this "technique for descent."

Though it was about 3000 feet to the valley floor, we managed to reach there safely with our trophy and to continue on to make camp that night. In the next two days of hunting Clyde had the satisfaction of bagging three nice black bear trophies. To me, the highlight of the trip was the climb for goat, the time spent on the windswept barren rocks up on the top.

In Alaska, many goat hunters have found the logger caulk boots to be the safest and most useful type footwear. When the hunter flattens the points of the caulks on a grindstone, they become a first rate safety device. In time and with considerable wear some of the caulks (pronounced *corks*) may require additional grinding to offer an even surface to the underside of the wearer's foot. Though goats hear well enough, sounds and falling rocks scarcely disturb them. A hunter wearing caulk or hob nailed boots can approach near enough for a fatal shot without the care necessary to make a quiet approach, such as is required in hunting most other trophy animals. Other dominant factors offset this single advantage in favor of the goat hunter.

When heavy snows first hit the goat country, the animals drop down to the top fringes of the timber line and feed in the alders. Their trails are easily discernible with binoculars, and weave in and out of the brush. Later, when the snow is crusted and will bear the weight of the goats, they can be observed again high up or on the tops of the mountains. Each little windswept ridge offers some food in the form of lichens and mosses. The coats of these mountaineers are perfect examples of nature's own insulation. The undercoat is of the very finest grade of wool protected by long guard hairs.

One year at the end of my fall mixed bag hunts when my non-resident hunters were all on the way back home, my thoughts turned to goat hunting for myself. My plans were to hunt a convenient ridge a short distance from home where one could almost always be sure of seeing a few goats. The route I chose for my climb was the most direct, but steepest part of the ridge. After a short climb through heavy alder, I crossed fresh grizzly tracks. I changed my course. Grizzlies are wonderful animals and rate at the top of many trophy lists, but I was after goat meat. I didn't care to be forced into killing a grizzly.

Veering off my original course, I continued my ascent. Again I crossed fresh grizzly tracks and again I changed course. In time I topped out at a good vantage point close to where I expected to see goats. Lying down on the rocks, I used my glasses. Almost directly below me I located two goats. As I started the sneak, the wind was right and there was sufficient cover to shield my approach. When in shooting range I chose the larger of the two and attempted to combine a spine and shoulder shot by holding at the top of his shoulder. The shot was low and missed the spinal column, but penetrated both shoulders. The goat staggered into the brush and disappeared from my view before I could fire the second shot. Quickly I followed. I was brought to a sudden stop as a here-to-fore unseen goat bounded in front of me to bar my way. Never before had I been challenged by a pugnacious goat. It was a nanny who had a kid cached behind her in the alders. The kid did not stay cached. It joined its mother and frantically leaped in circles around her. To allay their fears and permit the mother to go on her way without interference, I could do nothing but sit down, wait, and wonder if my wounded goat would escape due to this delay. The nanny shook her horns at me. She stamped her forefeet and bounded about, but seemed content to limit her pugnaciousness to these threats. Her fighting and protective spirit was most impressive. It is well known that goats are capable in defending themselves and have great courage, but it is not every day that one can witness it in such close quarters as I found myself that bleak October day.

My goat, when I caught up with it, was swaying on its feet. Another shot downed it but not until it had fallen off a low cliff and wedged itself tightly in a tangle of alders. The goat had traveled many yards with a bad wound. Yet he had made his way through a maze of alder and willow brush and never lost his footing, traveling on three legs. Such toughness and tenacity of life is remarkable. Pound for pound of body weight, in my opinion, a goat requires more killing and can absorb more punishment and shock than any other American game animal. Naturally a perfectly placed shot will kill goat quickly, but placing the perfect shot is often only a dream or just plain good luck.

Goats are not always the winner in fights for survival among the wild animals. Black bears, wonderful little animals that they are, do win out over the goat at times. Personally, I do not begrudge the blackie an occasional goat, nor the big brownie or grizzly a moose now and then, nor the wolves a few caribou. This is nature's plan. Naturalists throughout the world frown on elimination of any single species.

While hunting goat with an Illinois client we located a fine, shiny, black bear high on the mountain, but presenting an almost sure, successful stalk. With the exception of a slide area to cross, we had perfect cover to conceal our approach. My client, Sam Atkinson of McLeansboro, Illinois, shooting a scope-sighted .270, took his trophy quickly. Before we could reach the fallen animal, I spotted another blackie running across the slide farther down, and below us. It appeared that he was reluctant to leave some object that he may have been feeding upon. He must have been in plain sight all the while that we were concentrating on the higher bear. The gunfire had spooked him. I checked with my binoculars and discovered a dead goat. Leaving my packer behind to skin out Sam's bear and pack the hide back to camp, Sam and I took off in hot pursuit. He was a fine, large billy. The black bear had managed to tear out part of the back just above the shoulders. Too much of the cape and neck had been ripped apart to save the head and horns for a trophy.

Wonderingly, I back-tracked and found ample evidence to reconstruct the story of the fight. I found a little bear hair, but matted goat hair made a perfect trail to follow over the cliffs directly to the scene of the initial attack.

The goat had been bedded down in a thick clump of brush at the base of a small rock cliff. The clever blackie made a good sneak to the top of this cliff and, as the tracks showed, launched himself off into space onto the goat's back and neck. From here on the advantage was all on his side. The goat had an injury below his right eye which could well have caused his lack of vigilance. It was a suppurating wound which may have resulted from a fight or possibly from a flying rock in a slide. Whatever the cause, it may have been an act of mercy that this blackie completed. The goat might have suffered a lingering death.

Jack Seidensticker's one-shot kill was an anticlimax to the brush with calamity that came during the stalk.

Clyde Fogg brought three glossy blacks as well as a goat down from their vertical range on the Kenai.

Resident hunters and guides outfitting non-resident hunting parties find it advantageous to hunt both species of game, goat and black bear, simultaneously as both animals are found in the same range, often feeding within eyesight of each other. To the observer, the animals have worked out a truce between themselves with strict rules of conduct. The goats appear indifferent and unconcerned. The black bear, clown and actor that he is, hopes to appear likewise. If you were close enough to the bear you would see him stealing quick looks at the goat, all the while busily occupied with his digging, feeding, or other concern of the moment.

The goat is a confident and exceptionally courageous adventurer. He is never over-confident, but in his calm way is sure of each deliberated move. It may be a descent that looks impossible or it may be an ascent that you know is impossible as there are no footholds showing to the human eye. Mr. Goat carefully plans each move before he starts out. There is nothing headlong about the phlegmatic goat. Whereas sheep who may inhabit the same terrain will dash madly up and down sheer cliffs, they would be killed if they tried to follow a goat's progress. A mature goat is capable of reversing his direction on a narrow trail only wide enough for his body with a drop-off of possibly hundreds of feet. By the simple expedient of rearing up on his back legs, turning faceout to the drop-off, he can whirlabout like a dancer and drop on all fours again, turned safely in the opposite direction. Such maneuvers are breathtaking to watch and unforgettable to the few individuals who can be rewarded thus for frequenting the rugged peaks.

Alaskan goat hunting is confined to the coast ranges adjacent to salt water, which, of course, means that the hunter must be prepared to accept heavy precipitation and heavy fogs.

A goat trophy is one to be proud of. The mounted head requires little room and in almost every instance there remain memories of dangers, thrills, and unparalleled mountain beauty. My compliments to the mountain goat—Mountaineer Supreme. ■

In Southeastern Alaska the climb to goat range starts from tidewater, or preferably, from a high mountain lake.

Fisherman's Railroad

There were other fishermen besides our trio to load their gear aboard the Alaska Railroad baggage car.

By CHARLES J. KEIM

Reprinted from Alaska Sportsman® , March, 1959 (ALASKA® magazine)

Residents and tourists alike rapidly are discovering that a quick way to obtain good fishing in Alaska is to head for the "boondocks" aboard The Alaska Railroad which stretches 470.3 miles from Seward to Fairbanks through a land of great beauty and variety.

Bill mixed a few whitefish with his bag in addition to grayling and salmon.

Charles Ray is partial to grayling and picks out a couple for the pan.

Inevitably, the rapidly increasing population in this newest and largest state and the thousands of tourists who annually flock northward are beginning to depopulate many of the fishing streams close to the highways, but there's still plenty of good fishing for those who are willing to hike a ways from the roads or stay at a strategically located resort. The railroad is one of the answers for those who can't hike or lack the time to do so.

192

Four of us simply lacked the time to pack in one July when we decided on a week-end of fishing while summer session was going full blast at the University of Alaska. Members of our party were Dr. Robert R. Wiegman, university vice president; Dr. William K. Keller, head of the education department; Charles Ray, associate professor of education, and myself, professor of journalism.

We had spotted Indian River at Mile 270.0 on an earlier rail trip and had decided immediately to fish it and at the same time test the "Railroad for Fishermen" promotional brochure which states:

"Near the mainline north of Seward lie Kenai and Skilak Lakes and the famous Kenai and Russian Rivers. In the summer these waters abound in sea run salmon and Alaska's largest Dolly Varden and Rainbow trout.

"Trout from this Kenai Peninsula district often weigh between eight and ten pounds and are topped only by giant Mackinaw trout found in railbelt lakes. Attractive Wonder Lake, located in McKinley National Park, has a large population of Mackinaw.

"From Nancy Lake, Mile 180.7, north to the McKinley National Park boundary, is located a maze of lakes, streams and rivers loaded with fighting sport fish.

"From May until early June powerful Chinook salmon, weighing up to sixty pounds, invade this area. By June, Reds, Silvers and Pinks supplement a run that continues late into September.

"Nancy, Bear, and Reno lakes are usually good for Rainbow trout, Dolly Varden and Grayling. These creeks are also good: Big and Little Willow, Montana, Sheep, Troublesome, and Clear, as well as tributaries of the Talkeetna, Susitna, Kashwitna and Indian Rivers."

Though listed last on the brochure, Indian River was our first venture and it proved successful as these photographs will show. And we learned something else—merely tell the conductor where you want to get off and he'll stop the train; check the schedule to learn when it will be coming back, wave your shirt to the engineer who will answer with two quick toots on the horn when he sees you.

That is when you clamber aboard and watch the scenery as you anticipate how those fish will taste when you return home on the "Railroad for Fishermen." ■

What Kind Of Hunter Are You?

Some hunters like to take time out for some King crab "hunting."

Story and photos by HAL WAUGH

Reprinted from Alaska Sportsman® , March, 1962 (ALASKA® magazine)

The hunt is over and the sportsman is back in the swing of modern day living. Commuters, conferences, and appointments quickly replace the tree, trails, and sleeping bags. The first questions asked of the hunter returning from an African safari, an Indian shikari, or an Alaskan big game hunt invariably concern the size of his trophies.

"How big?" "Win an award?" The white hunter, guide, or outfitter is asked: "Get your dudes any big ones?"

I have wondered if we aren't losing something of value with this modern trend to outdo the other fellow, to get the largest or the most outstanding. Why wouldn't the questions: "Have a good time?" "Get any good pictures?" be more appropriate for the homecoming sportsman or returning professional hunter and guide?

In generalization, I think we may break down hunters into two classifications—the "Award or Rack" hunters and the "Fun" hunters. Roughly, each classification can again be divided into two groups. The

195

type "A" or "good" hunters and the type "B" or "less desirable hunters."

Award hunters, type B, may often be completely selfish and self-centered, seemingly interested only in "beating the other fellow" and getting something in the book if not an outright award. All too often a hunter in this group has very little background and training for the job he aspires to, and unfortunately does not have the mental stability necessary to compete with the semi-pro, Award hunter, type A, the experienced, determined fellow who will have fun and yet go home empty handed before he will shoot a "representative of the species," just to kill an animal.

Fun hunters, type B, can really make a guide "tear his hair" at times. Picture a hard working, ambitious guide who has planned for months for a certain hunt and may have flown in a cache of equipment and food in preparation for the coming hunt, to say nothing of miles and miles of hiking over muskeg or climbing up mountains, scouting out country . . . only to learn when his client reaches camp that he isn't too interested in serious hunting and very likely will not take advantage of the spike camps, or caches laboriously prepared for his hunt at considerable expense. Too often his physical condition is atrocious and though the client doesn't worry, the guide or outfitter may worry considerably about his own reputation. It is understandable if the guide feels that he isn't giving full value for money received, no matter how hard he tries, or how well qualified he may be in his chosen profession. A Fun, type B, client can be a real toughy to handle, but, fortunately, not too many clients of this group appear during a season.

Fun hunter, type A, can be a real joy to any outfitter. With reasonable preparation on the part of the guide, this man will enjoy himself, be a welcome addition to any camp, and go home completely revitalized and ready for the routine work-a-day world. Sportsmen from all age groups fall into this much desired clientele. Some young sportsmen enter the game with so much enthusiasm and zest that they almost overwhelm the guides. Actually, older men make up most of this group. They're fellows who have been around long enough to love the game and appreciate every moment—the conversation in the evenings, coffee, hotcakes and bacon in the mornings, sunrises and sunsets, unusual views, and every single head of game, fowl, and fish that is observed. When this Fun hunter, type A, collects an unusual or outstanding specimen, he really "hits the overhead," but if the trophy is just ordinary, he still enjoys the hunt, and life is pretty rewarding to the guide.

Any hunter is gratified to take a trophy which will win an award, but the price paid is often the sacrifice of many homey, memorable pleasures that could accompany the hunting trip.

Trophy heads must necessarily be rare. If they were obtainable in quantity they would lose much of their appeal to hunters. Many hunters strive for the outsize, but few obtain them.

As an outfitter I have been at least partially responsible for the ambitious attitude of many of my clients. An outfitter couldn't ask for better advertising than award wins for his clients. Naturally, I have encouraged selective hunting and thereby have spurred my repeat clients to try for the biggest ones. In doing so we have passed up many

Others like Charles Erwin Wilson, Jr. help round up some spruce grouse for the base camp cooking pot.

nice trophies. Later we may have been forced to take lesser trophies than those already rejected, or go home empty handed. Too, in our hunt for the big ones, we often have left no time for the simple pleasures of camp life. Small things that leave pleasant memories involve relaxation, but they are time consuming when every hour is important in serious hunting.

My client, an Award, type B hunter, and I were after Dall sheep, but goat which were to be found in the same region were high on my client's want list. The sheep came first, however, and nothing was supposed to interfere with our attempts to secure a trophy ram. Weather, sore leg muscles, blisters, or other game should not interrupt

197

our quest for the award winner, or for a trophy at least good enough for entry in the book.

We saw and passed up several goats. My client was well aware of his gamble, but his ambition to get the big ram was like a disease. He could think of nothing else. All the rams we were looking over were just ordinary animals with compact, gleaming white bodies and gray-amber curled headgear. All were beautiful, but not one was outsized. The mountain tops provided disagreeable vantage points in disagreeable weather. My hunter was earning my respect for his perseverance, but he wasn't having any fun. He tried to enter into the joking and conversation around camp in the evenings, but couldn't. He was too tired. He barely moved to eat and go to bed. While we were discussing the relative merits of Goldline, versus Perlon solid core climbing line, he would dreamily interject, "I wonder if I should have taken that third ram. How good do you think he was?" Usually his remarks were followed with groans and "don't know how I can get out of this sack in the morning, but call me early—groan, moan."

No, my hunter wasn't enjoying the hunt. The old type, around-the-camp fun and pleasure were missing. After we finally got his ram down, one for the book, he forgot his interest in sheep hunting. He quickly turned to goat hunting techniques. He became an avid goat hunter, but concentration wasn't enough. Friend hunter had no chance during the remainder of our hunt to take a good goat. After bitter self-condemnation my client resolved on our next hunt he would certainly take any desirable trophy when the opportunity presented itself and have more fun doing it—conversion from Award hunter, type B, to type A.

Although I have lived in close contact with moose for years and have conducted many moose hunts, I find the animal difficult to judge for trophy evaluation. Some claim that they can quickly and easily judge a moose for trophy score, but I take a dim view of their attitudes and I'm skeptical of their abilities.

Again, with an Award, type B hunter, on a hunt for a big moose, my client, the packer, and I passed up five bull moose and three bull caribou on the first day. I just couldn't be sure any one of those we saw was of award size, and there was too much pressure on me to get only, "one for the book." On the fifth day of our hunt after a long sneak to get in close and really scrutinize a fine, big bull moose, I told my client "take this one." The big fellow won an award and is now listed well up in the all-time records. A case in point for perseverance, you might say, but to this day I am not sure that two of the bulls we passed up would not have outscored the one my client finally put his sights on. Obviously, there was too much pressure on all three of us. We were nervous, apprehensive lest we take a less than trophy head.

We were glad when the hunt was over. It could have been so different had we not been faced constantly with the urge to get a prize winner. We were camped where moose and caribou were plentiful; we had a wide selection of delicious camp food; our tentage was of the best quality; and the scenery went begging for lack of appreciation and photographic interest.

Alaskan brown bear, Kodiak, brownie, or what have you in names, undoubtedly attract more attention and thus foster more stirring tales than any other animal in North America. Apparently every nimrod aspires to take home a huge Alaskan brown bear rug. I don't blame them, because in my opinion the big bear is the most attractive and interesting game animal in the world, with the possible exception of African elephant—and both will fight back.

On a bear hunt several years ago, Mr. Smith, a positive Fun, type A hunter, expressed no special yearning for an outsize bear. He merely wanted to bag a nice, acceptable specimen. Mr. Smith was a congenial companion, quick to call attention to his obvious inexperience in the game fields. Too, he daily mentioned that working behind a desk wasn't conducive to conditioning for fairly rugged hunting. We waited patiently for Mr. Smith to puff up the hills and all of us enjoyed the pleasure of his company. Every member of the crew was elated when we managed to get him one of the largest bears ever recorded by a non-resident hunter.

The story was different on another year and on a second try for big bear. In the interim, Mr. Smith had suddenly developed hunting instincts and abilities that apparently had lain dormant for his entire life. He had become an expert on his first major, two-week hunt—an undisputed Award, type B fellow. Too, he informed me on his return that he wanted a guide who could hunt from morning till night, and not waste a single precious moment. Also, he was now after what he termed, "Old Grandpa ... the largest bear that ever walked." What had happened to Mr. Smith, our friendly companion of the previous hunt? AWARDITIS had set in.

Without malice I assigned to Mr. Smith a guide who was noted for his indefatigable constitution and his yearning to see what was on the other side of the hill. The guide was a big, long geared fellow who stood 6' 5" tall. His hunting experience dated back to childhood days when he was first taken into the game fields by his dad and older brothers. Two weeks later when a tired, bedraggled Mr. Smith left camp with his second bear, he had the graciousness to call me aside and offer his apologies.

"What was I thinking of," he lamented, "when I foolishly asked for a guide who could hunt all day? You certainly gave me one." It had been a mistake, too, thinking of and looking for old Grandpa. "From now on," Smith vowed, "I'm going to have fun on my trips." Conversion to a fun hunter.

Some, like Sam Atkinson, re-live their hunt when they uncrate their trophies.

Extremely important factors influencing true award type hunting are the physical condition and ability of the hunter. Certain game species and regions call for a fairly high degree of physical ability. Goats are superb mountaineers and, more often than not, exact a stiff toll from their pursuers. Sheep normally are found in high, rather inaccessible mountain ranges that tax the limit and strength of able hunters.

Guided hunts are naturally costly and the average sportsman may be middle aged before he is established in his world of business and can afford a well managed, guided hunt. His waist line often expands at a rate equal to his bank account. Few of us care to mention that we are growing older and softer. The older hunters are frequently

200

travelers with world wide experience. Many become epicures, or, as Webster puts it, "given to dainty indulgence in pleasure of the table." The indulgence, coupled with the ability to judge good wines, just isn't of much value when you are balanced with a precarious foothold on a steep cliff or laboring up a mountain lugging a scope sighted rifle, binoculars dangling around your neck, and fighting for every lungful of oxygen.

Oddly enough, the mature and older hunters have as much or more enthusiasm for sheep and goat hunting as do the younger men. However, the older sportsmen do not have the steam left to do the ridge and mountain climbing necessary to get up in sheep or goat habitat, and then keep going. It is not my intention to exclude all older hunters from fascinating alpine sport in the high meadows because a very few older men are exceptional individuals, superior in stamina and ability to many young men.

Older men form a large core of the annual sheep hunting fraternity. Most of them expect to get one for the book, if not an outright award winner. There is no diplomatic way to tell a nice, friendly fellow, overweight from rich living, soft from lack of exercise, and short of hunting know-how that he should be happy and content if he should be fortunate enough to secure a legal ram at all. To ask for more is to encourage personal egotism and sometimes downright physical risk.

Of course there is a pleasure and satisfaction in standing on the award platform at the Museum of Natural History and receiving a certificate for some outstanding trophy. It might be better to accept such good fortune as just an extra wonderful something that resulted from a fun-filled hunt, rather than to make a concentrated effort to uncover the biggest trophy of all.

In Alaska we have areas that offer outstanding hunting, but very little chance for a true prize winner. Several locations I know will offer the hunter a choice of four or five species from one base camp. Ordinarily, the animals are average in size and good representatives of the species. Often the hunting is not difficult nor will it tax the older heart and out-of-condition hunter. When the hunter is not capable of hunting safely more than one or two of the available species, he can limit his hunting to the more easily bagged animals and have a whale of a good time doing so.

In the initial correspondence, the outfitter can recommend when to come and where to go to get the game and have the fun that a client wants . . . once the outfitter knows the physical condition, experience, and ambition of his prospective client.

Southeastern Alaska, for example, was once a drawing card for large numbers of sportsmen from all over the globe. These hunters came to Alaska not to win awards, but to enjoy the magnificent scenery, hospitality of a friendly people, fishing second to none in both salt and fresh water, and a fine selection of game to hunt. Species available include brown bear, grizzlies, black bear, goat, and Sitka blacktail deer. Added minor attractions are hair seal, sea lion, and multitudes of ducks and geese. The game is as plentiful as it was in former years, and moose, since introduced, can now be included in the selection.

Guides in southeastern Alaska have perfected hunting to a fine degree that older people can enjoy as thoroughly as the young and more vigorous. Using cruisers as a base camp, which can be moved easily to concentrations of game, the non-resident can live in comfort and even sleep while camp is moving. Canoes, fiberglass skiffs, dories, or whatever craft is efficient for the operation, are used to hunt the beaches and the heads of the many picturesque bays. True, the hunter is not likely to win a Boone and Crockett award, but he'll receive returns that are far more valuable to him.

We find many of these favorable conditions on the Kenai Peninsula, Kodiak Island, and the Alaskan Peninsula and certainly we know that each of these three districts offers attractive possibilities for true award winners. Kenai has long deserved a reputation as the top producer of outsize moose and in recent years with a limited sheep season, is again ringing the gong with sheep. Goats, of course, have always been plentiful. The word "KODIAK" is magic to bear hunters, unquestionably the ultimate in bear hunting, but suitable, too, for the Fun hunter.

The Alaska Peninsula, that wild and stormy piece of property, has kept the Kodiak hunters on their toes always, to maintain the spot at the top of the ladder with big bear. In recent years, moose, and very large ones, are showing up in the award lists. As if this were not enough, caribou are quite plentiful, and these trim, compact animals carry an outsize set of head gear.

Interior Alaska, particularly the Alaska Range, a vast sprawling mass of mountains topped by Mt. McKinley at 20,300 feet and extending in a semi-circle for over 500 miles, can show the hunter, hiker, fisherman, or sightseer just about anything he may elect to accomplish. The Award hunter can aim for moose, sheep, caribou, or grizzly and could win with any one of the four species, but the "Fun" hunter has an even wider range of activities available.

Guides do not encourage hunters to take one of each type trophy available, but from the list of four or five animals the hunter can select one or two or three types that fit well with either his personal choice or his physical limitations. Enjoyment, beauty, and satisfaction are here for the taking. A well managed, guided hunt, is sure to send the sportsman home in safety with a trophy or two; memories of innumerable grayling caught, released or retained as needed for the pan; a ptarmigan or two shot and eaten, and plentiful amounts of succulent wild game chops and steaks. Interior Alaska is a land with a multitude of game with endless opportunities for photography. A wise selection for a hunter in any age group, whether he is an Award or a Fun hunter.

Some like to take time out for fishing.

Now it's to figure out ways to cook their catches.

To the far north, beyond the Arctic Circle, Alaska has the mighty Brooks Range extending from the Bering Strait across the state to the Canadian border. The Brooks is a mysterious and exotic mountain system—a real privilege to see, explore, and hunt. The Brooks, like southeastern Alaska, interior Alaska, and the Kenai Peninsula, provides a hunter with a diversified selection of game including thousands of barren ground caribou, moose from the southern extremities to within sight of the Arctic Ocean, grizzly bear, black bear, and a heavy concentration of the beautiful white sheep. These too, might not be trophies for "the book," but few hunters who go there can resist its spell to the point they'll virtually forget all about "the book." An especially good area for the Fun hunter.

There are many dedicated hunters whose main ambitions are to bag only top drawer specimens. Award hunters, type A, the real "purists" of the hunting world. It is an unwritten law among this group that no animal be taken unless he is in the highly selected few that will rank well up in the record book. This assembly of sportsmen concentrates on one species only during an entire hunt. Men of this caliber deserve commendation because they contribute greatly to our wildlife knowledge and in many instances are in a position to have a strong voice in politics and appropriation measures which are so vital to game management. They are game conservationists who pass up the young virile male for the monarch whose years on earth will soon come to a natural end. Selective hunting by such a minority group can have no bearing on the normal kill each season. Contrary to the attitude of meat hunters and the often narrow minded public, such a group of

204

trophy hunters is vital to the successful hunting of future generations. Nevertheless, the average hunter must recognize that it is not necessary or advisable for him to attempt to imitate these semi-professional trophy hunters in order to enjoy the wonderfully productive hunts almost anywhere on earth where hunters are popping a cap.

Small and restricted areas, which for reason of isolation and good food and living conditions produce the highest scoring trophies of certain species, can stand only a given amount of heavy hunting pressure before the quality of the trophies starts to drop. Our game management program faces disaster when pilots who must keep their aircraft busy, or unscrupulous professional hunters and outfitters who feel they have to corner every bit of the non-resident traffic possible, persist in over hunting the few limited award winning areas.

A solution appears simple to many thoughtful and concerned observers. Let us hunt the vast general game areas. Experienced outfitters know many small isolated areas all over Alaska that may in many cases produce award winners, but are certain to offer visiting sportsmen first class, fun-filled hunts. The sportsman could really enjoy the hunt of his life if he would de-emphasize the seeming importance of getting one for the book.

Now that the prime necessity for hunting to obtain food no longer is of consequence, the field of pleasure and satisfaction the sportsman can derive from well managed hunting trips is practically unlimited if he will avoid "Awarditis."

After many years of outfitting and guiding, I guess that if I had to make the choice between Award or Fun hunters, I'd put my laurels on the Fun, type A hunter and urge others to give more thought to enjoying the little pleasures of camp life: the early morning coffee, the tantalizing smell of frying bacon, the beautiful panoramic view of untramped mountains extending on and on but centered around a single cow moose feeding from the bottom of a lake.

Spend some time with your camera recording daily events. Take it easy on the old pump. You may want it for a long time to enjoy hunting to the fullest with little emphasis on "the book" and more on the simple by-products in the world of outdoors. ■